UPRISING SHAKES
Iran Regime's Foundations

A Significant Step Toward Eventual Downfall

Published by

NATIONAL COUNCIL OF RESISTANCE OF IRAN
U.S. REPRESENTATIVE OFFICE (NCRI-US)

Uprising Shakes Iran Regime's Foundations
A Significant Step Toward Eventual Downfall

Copyright © National Council of Resistance of Iran – U.S. Representative Office, 2019.

All rights reserved. No part of this monograph may be used or reproduced in any manner whatsoever without written permission except in the case of brief quotations embodied in articles or reviews.

First published in 2019 by
National Council of Resistance of Iran - U.S. Representative Office (NCRI-US),
1747 Pennsylvania Ave., NW, Suite 1125, Washington, DC 20006

ISBN-10 (paperback): 1-944942-36-X
ISBN-13 (paperback): 978-1-944942-36-6

ISBN-10 (e-book): 1-944942-37-8
ISBN-13 (e-book): 978-1-944942-37-3

Library of Congress Control Number: 2019919802

Library of Congress Cataloging-in-Publication Data

National Council of Resistance of Iran - U.S. Representative Office.
Uprising Shakes Iran Regime's Foundations
1. Iran. 2. Human Rights. 3. Protests. 4. Democracy. 5. Middle East

First Edition: November 2019
Second Edition: December 2019
Third Edition: December 2019
Printed in the United States of America

These materials are being distributed by the National Council of Resistance of Iran-U.S. Representative Office. Additional information is on file with the Department of Justice, Washington, D.C.

Table of contents

5   **Executive summary**

9   **Chapter 1 — Events on the ground**
- Slogans
- Impacted cities and provinces
- Khamenei orders massive crackdown
- Over 1,500 killed and still counting
- People react to barbaric crackdown

25   **Chapter 2 — Regime's stance on the MEK's role in the uprising**
- Overview
- In their own words

35   **Chapter 3 — Suppression and the regime's crimes**
- Overview
- Red alert mobilization and organizational chart
- "Controlling Riots and Protests"
- Command and Control Headquarters
- Wireless communications reveal regime's inability to curb protests
- Massacre in Mahshahr

51   **Chapter 4 — Regime officials involved in suppression of the uprising**
- Introduction
- Who's in charge?
- Tehran Province
- Kurdistan Province
- Khuzestan Province
- Kermanshah Province

- Fars Province
- Isfahan Province
- Alborz Province

69   **Chapter 5 — Main takeaways of the November uprising**

73   **Chapter 6 — What should be done?**

75   **Appendix: Partial list of those fallen for freedom**

85   **List of publications**

91   **About the NCRI-US**

Executive summary

This manuscript examines the nationwide uprising that erupted on November 15, 2019 and spread to over 180 cities in all 31 provinces of Iran. Although the unrest was sparked by a gasoline price hike, by as much as 300 percent, the protests rapidly expanded and changed focus, concentrating on the nature of the regime.

From the first day, the regime resorted to sheer violence and State Security Forces (SSF) declared a state of red alert, whereby the SSF handed over responsibility for suppressing the uprising to the IRGC, and SSF forces were put under IRGC command.

Protesters soon called for regime change by chanting "death to Khamenei," "death to Rouhani," and "death to dictatorship" as they confronted the repressive forces. According to the regime's own officials, dozens of centers of repression such as the Islamic Revolutionary Guard Corps (IRGC), Bassij, and police headquarters were attacked, after the regime started to fire live ammunition at demonstrators.

In addition, over one thousand state-run banks, mostly owned by the regime's Supreme Leader, Ali Khamenei, and the IRGC, were attacked. Iranians see these financial institutions as plunderers of their wealth and resources, whose main mission is to fund the instruments of repression inside Iran and terrorism abroad. For example, Bank Melli, the largest bank in Iran with over 3,000 branches, and Bank Mellat (owned by Khamenei's SETAD) with over 1,600 branches, were major targets. Both have already been designated as terrorist entities by the U.S. Treasury. Khamenei, whose representative offices were also attacked by the youth, was himself sanctioned by the Treasury Department.

The regime cut off the internet on the second day to disrupt communications between protesters and prevent reports of the scale and intensity of the uprising, as well as of the atrocities committed by the IRGC and SSF from getting to the outside world. The shutdown lasted for several days before service was partially resumed in some areas.

> **The regime cut off the internet on the second day to disrupt communications between protesters and prevent reports of the scale and intensity of the uprising, as well as of the atrocities committed by the IRGC and SSF from getting to the outside world.**

The Iranian regime confronted the growing protests with bullets, using both snipers and in many cases shooting protesters at point-blank range. It deployed its multitude of repressive agencies and capabilities. Consequently, the latest casualty figures as of the publication of this report exceed 1,500 dead, nearly half of whom have been identified by the Iranian Resistance. Over 4,000 were wounded and at least 12,000 arrested in some 190 towns and cities.

The resistance has also identified 92 of the officials who had leading roles in the violent murder and detention of protesters in the seven provinces which were the scenes of the most significant, widespread, and pervasive protests.

The book also highlights the role of the main Iranian opposition movement, the Mujahedin-e Khalq (MEK) and their Resistance units and councils, as conceded by many major regime officials.

The key characteristics of the nationwide uprising which, by all indications, has shaken the regime to its foundations are:

1. The uprising showed that overthrow of the regime is attainable, as the public targeted the main symbols of repression, theft, and corruption.

2. The people consider the regime and all its factions as illegitimate. Iranians are ready to pay the price to unseat the ayatollahs.

3. The utter weakness of the regime, manifested by its barbaric and rampant use of brute force as well as its shutting down of the internet, was on display.

4. The gains of the uprising are irreversible; no matter how deep or wide the state suppression, the unrest will persist.

5. The role of the organized opposition exemplified by the Resistance units and councils formed by the MEK was key and will continue until the regime is brought down.

> **The gains of the uprising are irreversible; no matter how deep or wide the state suppression, the unrest will persist.**

The Iranian Resistance has called on the international community to take the following measures:

- The slaughter of protesters is a clear case of a crime against humanity. Therefore, the United Nations Security Council, and governments should take urgent action to halt the killings and suppression and secure the release of political prisoners.
- Investigative missions must be sent to Iran to evaluate the scope of the crimes and examine the cases of those killed, wounded and/or detained.
- The leaders of the regime, e.g., Supreme Leader Ali Khamenei and President Hassan Rouhani, must be held accountable for crimes against humanity.

- The United States should sanction Western companies that aid the Iranian regime with the sale and provision of services and products that enable it to monitor, control, and block internet access by Iranian citizens. While adopting all measures necessary to diminish and disable the regime's capacity to block internet traffic, the United States should provide safe, secure, and uninterruptible internet access to Iran's people, including the protesters.

- It is time for the world to recognize the right of the Iranian people to change the repressive regime and establish a democratic, pluralistic and non-nuclear republic based on separation of religion and state.

Chapter 1
Events on the ground

Background

The flames of the recent Iran uprising were initially lit on November 15, 2019, after the sudden tripling of gasoline prices. At first, people in several cities chanted slogans against the fuel price hike. For example, in the city of Behbahan (Khuzestan Province), "gasoline becomes more expensive, the poor become poorer" was among the first slogans. In Ahvaz (also in Khuzestan Province), protestors chanted "honorable Ahvazi, turn off your car." It did not take long, however, for the slogans to morph into calls for rejection of the regime in its entirety. In subsequent hours, gasoline-related slogans took on a secondary role, and instead people chanted slogans against the regime's Supreme Leader, Ali Khamenei, and President, Hassan Rouhani, while attacking centers of suppression, theft, and particularly those affiliated with the Islamic Revolutionary Guard Corps (IRGC). This report offers an overview of the developments that unfolded during the November 2019 uprising.

Scenes of the November 2019 uprising across Iran

Slogans

Some of the slogans chanted on the first day of the uprising were against increases in gasoline prices, including "I will no longer buy gasoline" or "Oil revenues are lost, spent on Palestine." Most of the slogans, however, had political overtones, such as "Rouhani, resign, resign" and "An Iranian will die but never accept humiliation," which was heard in the northeastern city of Mashhad.

From the second day onwards, the following slogans were chanted:

- "Death to Khamenei"
- "Death to dictator"
- "Death to Rouhani"
- "Our enemy is right here; they lie when they say it's America"
- "Our idiot leader is a source of shame"
- "Death to Bassiji"
- "Dictator, shame on you, let go of the country"

The graffiti reads: Death to Khamenei

- "Rouhani, shame on you, let go of the country"
- "Canons, tanks, flames, mullahs must be killed"
- "Leave Syria alone; think about us instead"
- "Not Gaza, nor Lebanon, I will sacrifice my life for Iran"
- "Iranians, enough is enough; show your dignity"
- "Imprisoned university students must be freed"
- "Don't be afraid, don't be afraid; we are all together"
- "The pressures are breaking our backs, but we will overcome"
- "Rouhani, shame on you, hands out of our pockets"
- "We've shed tears of blood for forty years; it's enough, we will stand up"
- "Enough slavery! our people have had it"

As manifested in these slogans, there was no doubt that protestors were demanding the elimination of the regime and its core pillars.

UPRISING SHAKES IRAN REGIME'S FOUNDATIONS

Impacted cities and provinces

The protests began in cities across Khuzestan Province in the west. They quickly spread to dozens of other municipalities in all of Iran's provinces. Major cities that saw extensive protests and clashes include: Tehran, Karaj, Shahriar, Isfahan, Shiraz, Tabriz, Ardebil, Orumiyeh, Rasht, Sari, Babol, Kermanshah, Javanroud, Kamyaran, Sanandaj, Neyshabour, Saveh, Birjand, Nourabad Momseni, Marvdasht, Bojnourd, Andimeshk, Behshahr, Nour, Boushehr, Mahshahr, Chabahar, Gachsaran, Abadan, Behbahan, Bandar Rig, Kangan, Iranshahr, Sirjan, Khorramshahr, Marivan, Eslamabad, Gilan Gharb, Jarrahi, Koureh, Qaemshahr, Mehrshahr, Pol-e Dokhtar, Fardis (Karaj), Islamshahr, and Baharestan.

Regime officials and state-run media outlets have admitted that the uprising encompassed at least 165 cities and towns.

The map of Iran showing locations of the November 2019 uprising.

All of Iran's cities with populations of one million or more — Tehran, Mashhad, Isfahan, Karaj, Shiraz, Tabriz, Ahvaz, Kermanshah and Khorramabad — were scenes of major protests and clashes.

Among the impacted cities, several saw some of the most ferocious confrontations between the people and the regime's suppressive forces. These include: Shiraz, Mahshahr, Behbahan, Isfahan, Kermanshah, Karaj, Eslamshahr, Marivan, Shahriar, Fardis, Shahrak-e Taleqan in Mahshahr, Khorramshahr, and towns in the vicinity of Tehran and Karaj.

> **All of Iran's cities with populations of one million or more — Tehran, Mashhad, Isfahan, Karaj, Shiraz, Tabriz, Ahvaz, Kermanshah and Khorramabad — were scenes of major protests and clashes.**

Khamenei orders massive crackdown

From the very first day of protests, repressive forces of the theocratic regime used lethal force and live ammunition to, per Khamenei's directive, mercilessly crackdown on protesters.

On Friday evening, November 15, 2019 when the protests erupted, the State Security Force (SSF) opened fire on a demonstration by the people of Sirjan (south-central

UPRISING SHAKES IRAN REGIME'S FOUNDATIONS

The regime's repressive forces firing from the rooftop of the Justice Department building of the city of Javanrood, Kermanshah Province.

Iran), killing Ruhollah Nazari-Fat'h-abad (aged 37) and wounding many protesters. The suppressive forces shot Mr. Nazari in the head at Naft (Oil) Square, outside the city's oil depot, killing him instantly. Scores of protesters were wounded, so many that local hospitals could not accommodate them. Many were hospitalized in Kerman's Seyyed Ol-Shohada hospital. Enraged residents set fire to a petrol station and clashed with SSF agents.

Numerous cases have been documented showing that the regime's repressive forces, particularly the Islamic Revolutionary Guards Corps (IRGC), had deployed snipers to fire at demonstrators from the government buildings' roof tops.

On December 6, UN High Commissioner for Human Rights Michelle Bachelet issued a report stating, "Verified video footage indicates severe violence was used against protesters, including armed members of security forces shooting from the roof of a justice department building in one city, and from helicopters in another... We have also received footage which appears to show security forces shooting unarmed demonstrators from behind while they were running away, and shooting others directly in the face and vital organs – in other words shooting to kill. These are clear violations of international norms and standards on the use of force, and serious violations of human rights."

In one of the worst incidents, which took place on November 18, the High Commissioner said her Office had received information partially corroborating reports that "Iranian security forces used machine guns against protesters in Jarahi

Images captured from a harrowing film shows an SSF agent shooting a protester from close range.

> "We have also received footage which appears to show security forces shooting unarmed demonstrators from behind while they were running away, and shooting others directly in the face and vital organs – in other words, shooting to kill."

Square in Mahshahr – including against people fleeing the area and people hiding in nearby reed-beds," killing many people.

In addition, Amnesty International said, "Extensive video footage verified and analysed by Amnesty International's Digital Verification Corps shows security forces shooting at unarmed protesters."

"This alarming death toll is further evidence that Iran's security forces went on a horrific killing spree," said Philip Luther, Research and Advocacy Director for the Middle East and North Africa at Amnesty International.

> **"This alarming death toll is further evidence that Iran's security forces went on a horrific killing spree."**

"Harrowing testimony from eyewitnesses suggests that, almost immediately after the Iranian authorities massacred hundreds of those participating in nationwide protests, they went on to orchestrate a wide-scale clampdown designed to instil fear and prevent anyone from speaking out about what happened," Luther added.

According to information gathered by Amnesty International, "Families of victims have been threatened and warned not to speak to the media, or to hold funeral ceremonies for their loved ones. Some families are also being forced to make extortionate payments to have the bodies of their loved ones returned to them."

Two eyewitness accounts are most chilling. An eyewitness from Behbahan (Khuzestan Province) reporting to the MEK said, "The names of martyrs of Behbahan you have announced are all correct, but you have only named eight. More than 20 were martyred whom I myself counted, but could not take counting any more. Could not look at all those corpses. After November 18, it was no longer only their snipers shooting at protesters, they (repressive forces) just indiscriminately opened fire on people. I witnessed more than 10 protesters whose brains were scattered on the pavement." The eyewitness added, "A protester named Alafchi (last name) was hit with a barrage of machine gun fire so bad that his leg was cut off and he then bled to death. Whoever got close to him was hit by snipers. Three protesters went toward him to pull him out, but all three were shot in the head and died."

A staff of a medical clinic in Sadra township outside Shiraz also reported to the MEK that: "On the evening of November 16, several security agents came to the clinic and effectively took all the staff hostage, constantly threatening them with

Gorgan

Several members of the IRGC, some in plainclothes, firing at an unarmed protester in northern city of Gorgan at point blank range, while anther attacking him with an axe.

Gorgan

their guns. Until 11 pm of November 17 when the last batch of killed and wounded were brought in, 29 protesters had been killed, the majority of them with gunshot wounds to their head, neck and upper body. Ninety percent of the wounded were brought in by people with their motor bikes. All wounded were laid on the cold floor in the hospital hallways. Four of the wounded later died. My estimate is that we had between 150–160 wounded, maybe more."

On November 17, in Fardis County of Karaj (4th most populated city of Iran), the regime's agents, using Kalashnikovs, fired at demonstrators from rooftops. The protestors used stones, sticks, and whatever tools at their disposal to confront suppressive forces and to defend themselves.

Many reports suggested that the regime resorted to deploying Afghan proxy forces called the Fatemiyoun, formed to fight the regime's proxy war in Syria, against the local population.

None of the regime's repressive measures, and even the massacre in Mahshahr, could not stop the innocent people from continuing their protest; to the contrary, the more the regime killed, the more determined the people became.

Over 1,500 killed and still counting

Due to major interruptions in internet access and the regime's near total news blackout on the scale of the crackdown, the casualty figures and other statistics representing the utter brutality of the attempt to put down the uprising are being updated regularly, sometimes more than once a day. As of December 15, 2019, the casualty reports compiled from inside Iran, mostly provided by the MEK's resistance network, are:

- Number of impacted provinces: **31** (all of Iran's provinces)
- Number of impacted towns and cities: **191**
- Number of martyrs: **over 1500**
- Number of wounded: **over 4,000**
- Number of detainees: **over 12,000**
- Number of martyrs identified to date: **724** (see Appendix)

In view of the enormous scale of the uprising, eventually spreading to over 190 towns and cities, and townships, and the fearful regime's scrambling to prevent its overthrow, two days after the uprising, Khamenei personally and publicly came forward to order the suppression of the protests. Rouhani immediately followed, echoing his orders to suppress the public. Other regime officials supported their comments. Thus began a wave of slaughter.

Meanwhile, the internet blackout made the flow of information extremely difficult. The French daily *Le Monde* quoted Reporters without Borders, writing:

(Left): Newly dug graves for martyrs in the western city of Marivan in Kurdistan Province.
(Right): Brothers Mahmoud and Mehrdad Dashti Nia were shot and killed by security forces in the southwestern city of Behbahan in Khuzistan Province.

"After the internet shutdown, the threat of a bloodbath grows." According to one report, at least 118 injured protestors were being treated at four hospitals, including Sajjad hospital, Madani hospital, and Alborz hospital in Karaj and a hospital in Shahriar.

The latest figures compiled as of December 15, 2019 by the Iranian Resistance put the number of martyrs at over 1,500, but the real figures are believed to be much higher. The martyrs are mostly young adults and teen-agers, many of them shot in the head and chest. The regime has used various ploys to conceal the actual casualty figures. In many cases, the suppressive forces did not hand over the bodies of the dead to their families and even refused taking them to the coroner's office, and instead buried them in unknown locations.

People react to barbaric crackdown

After the regime started to fire live ammunition at demonstrators, killing and wounding many, defiant protesters reacted to the barbaric crackdown and attacked

UPRISING SHAKES IRAN REGIME'S FOUNDATIONS

Mellat Bank branches, whose main shareholder is Khamenei's SETAD, was a main target of protesters' wrath. The bank is designated as terrorist by the U.S. Treasury.

centers of repression such as the Islamic Revolutionary Guard Corps (IRGC), Bassij, and police headquarters.

In addition, over 1,000 state-run banks and financial institutions owned by the Supreme Leader, Ali Khamenei, and the IRGC, were attacked. People consider these financial institutions as plunderers of their wealth whose main mission is to fund the instruments of repression in Iran and terrorism abroad.

The targeted banks listed below have been designated as terrorist entities (Specially Designated Global Terrorists or SDGT) by the U.S. Treasury. For example, Bank Melli, Iran's largest bank with 3,100 branches, and Bank Mellat (owned by Khamenei's SETAD) with over 1,500 branches, Ansar Bank (owned by the IRGC) with 1,100 branches, Parsian Bank (main beneficiaries are Khamenei's SETAD and the IRGC) with 350 branches, Tejarat Bank (main shareholders are IRGC and Khamenei's Astan-e Ghods Razavi) with 1,500 branches, Saderat Bank (IRGC a shareholder) with 2,300 branches, and Sina Bank (owned by Khamenei's

Mostazafan Foundation) with over 250 branches, are all SDGT blacklisted, and were all major targets of the protesters. Another bank attacked, Pasargad, with over 350 branches, is also sanctioned by the U.S. Treasury, and is largely owned by the IRGC.

Khamenei, whose representative offices were also attacked by the youth, was himself sanctioned by the Treasury Department, along with his offices.

Fundamentally, all of the centers that were attacked and torched were affiliated with the IRGC or the Khamenei machinery and apparatus. Chain stores linked to the IRGC, IRGC-affiliated banks, suppressive forces' vehicles, Bassij centers, offices of mullahs affiliated with Khamenei, and government buildings were among the other targets. People also destroyed or set fire to large posters of Khamenei and those of his predecessor, Khomeini.

> **Fundamentally, all of the centers that were attacked and torched were affiliated with the IRGC or the Khamenei machinery and apparatus.**

Statistics and figures announced by the regime itself reveal a portion of the real scope of the damages. The state-run *Iran* daily reported:

- In only three days, damages worth an equivalent of at least 7.5% of the annual proceeds from gas price hikes were inflicted;
- 180 gas stations, 450 banks in 4 cities, and 80 branches of IRGC-affiliated chain stores were damaged.

The state-run *Etemad* newspaper wrote that youth in Shiraz had set 76 banks on fire. It added that "in 4 days, $1.5B USD in damages were inflicted on the nation's economy."

UPRISING SHAKES IRAN REGIME'S FOUNDATIONS

Bank Melli, Iran's largest bank with 3,325 branches and designated as terrorist (SDGT) by the U.S. Treasury, was a key target.

Sina Bank branches, owned by the Khamenei-affiliated Mostazafan Foundation, were extensively targeted by the protesters. Sina Bank has been designated by the U.S. Treasury as a terrorist entity.

The state-affiliated Rouydad-24 news agency said on November 21: "A knowledgeable source in the banking sector says that from November 15 to date, more than 1,000 bank branches have been damaged. Statistics regarding some of the damages are as follows: 120 Mellat Bank branches, 100 Maskan Bank branches, and 20 Pasargad Bank branches."

On November 24, Mullah Mojtaba Zolnour, Chairman of the National Security and Foreign Policy Committee of the regime's Majlis, said on state-run television (Network 5): "The enemy had planned to foment this crisis in the country around the end of January or early February of next year. We are informed that what happened (gas price hike) brought that plan forward and so they hurried and stepped up their efforts to exploit the situation. The Supreme Leader put out this fire...

"Well, these people were well-trained... For example, on Sunday, November 17, we had 147 clashes just in Tehran... Throughout the country, we had 800 clashes in just one day, forcing us to divide the strength of our forces.

"Many were identified. Some arrested. One of their methods to excite the people was utilizing the killed protesters... I have to point out here that shutting down the internet following the Supreme Leader's decision and remarks was very helpful in spoiling this pre-planned, organized scheme and wrapping up this unrest."

Interior Minister Abdolreza Rahmani Fazli admitted on November 26 that: "We were engulfed in more serious crisis in five provinces. The most damages were inflicted in Mallard, Baharestan, Quds, and Islamshahr ...On Saturday, incidents and clashes erupted in 100 locations in Tehran... More than 50 law-enforcement, military, and security bases were attacked. Some 500 protesters were moving on the radio & television, but our forces thwarted them."

Yadollah Javani, the IRGC's Deputy for Political Affairs also acknowledged the unparalleled extent and intensity of this round of unrest in respect to the 2009 and 2018 protests. On November 29, he said: "These incidents — so widespread and so extensive — were unprecedented in the 40-year history of the Islamic Revolution. What happened in the final days of Aban (mid-November) was a far-reaching, new phenomenon. Although we had seen similar incidents, such as attacking and torching Bassij bases, banks and government centers during the 2009 and 2018 revolts, they were nevertheless much smaller than the recent incidents. The events on Saturday and Sunday were extensive and continued in 29 provinces and hundreds of cities. Isfahan was one of the provinces where protests and clashes occurred in 110 locations. As for crowds, Isfahan came in third after Fars and Tehran provinces."

Chapter 2
Regime's stance on the MEK's role in the uprising

Overview

A cursory look at the statements and positions declared by the regime's leaders and state-run media clearly shows that Resistance units of the MEK were at the core of the uprising. These Resistance units were formed several years ago and have spread throughout the country since. They have a wealth of experience gained on the ground and through thousands of acts of protest.

Just two days after the onset of the uprising, the regime's Supreme Leader, Ali Khamenei, took to the pulpit on November 17 to set the stage for a crackdown, unprecedented in barbarity, before, as later suggested by many of his officials, the protesters could bring down his regime. A main portion of his speech was dedicated to characterizing the activists, chanting "down with dictator, down with Khamenei" in towns and cities across all 31 provinces of Iran, as "thugs" and "foreign mercenaries." Witnessing an all-out people's revolt unfolding right before his eyes, Khamenei, like all other dictators nearing the end, justified shedding the demonstrators' blood by demonizing them. His desperate ploy was parroted by other regime officials, including Rouhani.

Khamenei said: "In the course of such incidents, usually thugs, spiteful individuals and unsavory people enter the scene... You see that over the past two days, the two nights and one day, in which these incidents happened, all of the world's centers of evil have encouraged these actions against us. From the evil and wicked family of the Pahlavi dynasty to the wicked and criminal collective of the hypocrites (the regime's derogatory reference to the Mujahedin-e Khalq, MEK), they are constantly encouraging and inviting people on social networks and elsewhere to conduct these evil acts."

In their own words

According to the IRGC-affiliated Fars news agency, Hossein Ashtari, the Commander of State Security Forces (SSF), said: "Our investigations show that behind the scenes, anti-revolutionary organizations and the MEK led these movements. The country's security and law enforcement entities have identified these individuals, and God willing, they will be punished for their actions at the right time." (November 17)

The speaker of the regime's Majlis (parliament), Ali Larijani, said: "After hearing the profound and expedient words of Your Excellency (Khamenei), members of the Majlis consider it imperative to follow the path directed by Your Excellency, and we must coordinate more in order to deprive America, the MEK and anti-revolutionary stooges the opportunity to create chaos in the country." (Farhang Radio, November 18)

The head of the regime's Judiciary, Ebrahim Raisi, said: "In the face of offences involving troublemakers and those affiliated with anti-revolutionary elements and infiltrators who, in line with the enemy's desires, have targeted the security of

Protesters gathered in towns and cities in all 31 of Iran's provinces.

the people and society, please act with firmness and implement legal actions in coordination with state security and law enforcement forces." (Mizan News Agency, November 17)

Rouhani's spokesperson, Ali Rabei, said: "The behavior of the protestors is wholly consistent with the policies of old terrorists that we had in our country (i.e. MEK). For years and through terrorist operations, they have been waiting for Iran's will to break." (Khabar News TV, November 18)

> **Hossein Ashtari, the Commander of State Security Forces (SSF): "Our investigations show that behind the scenes, anti-revolutionary organizations and the MEK led these movements."**

UPRISING SHAKES IRAN REGIME'S FOUNDATIONS

The rebellious youth carry a fellow protester severely wounded by the regime's security forces' gunfire during the November 2019 uprising in Shiraz.

A member of the regime's Assembly of Experts and former Intelligence Minister, Mohammad Mohammadi Reyshahri, said: "The riots were not carried out by the people. The torching of the people's belongings and the destruction that happened were done by the MEK and anti-revolutionaries. People do not set fire to their own assets. The MEK was planning for riots for several months. They were quickly identified and their ranks were separated from those of the people." (Defa Press, November 18)

Sarcastically responding to Rouhani downplaying the size of the protests, Faezeh Hashemi, daughter of the regime's former president Ali Akbar Hashemi Rafsanjani, said: "Mr. Rouhani, if the number of protestors is so low, why have you shut down the internet? What is the reason for such treatment?" (Jamaran website, November 20)

Hassan Rouhani, the regime's President, said: "It became clear that the rioters were small in numbers. However, the rioters were organized, had plans, and were armed. They were acting completely on the basis of plans designed by the region's reactionary forces, the Zionists, and Americans." (Rouhani's official website, November 20)

The spokesperson for the Majlis Presiding Board, Assadollah Abbasi, said: "Ali Shamkhani, secretary of the Supreme National Security Council, said at a closed-

A police station, tasked with suppressing public unrest, was targeted by the protesters.

door meeting of the Majlis that a number of individuals who provoked people in the streets had been identified. It has become clear that they are in contact with the MEK. They were some of the hoodlums of the region who got paid to create chaos." (ILNA, November 17)

A Majlis deputy from Malayer said: "The Islamic Republic has been able to establish sustained security in Iraq and Syria. It will never succumb to the MEK's actions. The people of Iran, who remember enormous sacrifices, will never allow the blood of the martyrs to be trampled upon and will not support their actions. Therefore, they will not align themselves with the MEK and thugs." (Fars News Agency, November 17)

The head of the IRGC's paramilitary Bassij force, Gholamreza Soleimani, said: "The MEK have cells (units) in our country. And in other countries, too, agents and the MEK who are tied to America damage the public's interests." (Tabnak website, November 18)

The state-run daily *Jomhouri Eslami* reported on November 18 that "the commander of the IRGC Fajr Corps in Fars province says that the leaders of the riots had ties to the MEK."

Vatan-e Emrouz daily wrote: "The methods employed by the core units of the recent incidents show that these individuals were completely trained and, unlike many

UPRISING SHAKES IRAN REGIME'S FOUNDATIONS

Protesters prepare to confront the regime's repressive forces in the central city of Isfahan on November 16.

of the people who were surprised by the sudden jump in gasoline prices, these individuals were ready for such circumstances. The IRGC's public relations office in Alborz said in a statement that 150 of the leaders who disrupted security in the province had been identified and arrested." (November 17)

Jomhouri Eslami daily wrote in its editorial on November 20: "The scale of the destruction was so vast and the actions were carried out so professionally that it was obvious that a well-trained and well-equipped network was at work, which had financial and strong intelligence support. After the passing of two or three days, it is now clear that this assessment was correct, and the destruction and evil acts were completely organized. The rebels, in groups of several people, went to predetermined locations and were guided by a defined command center, and resorted to destruction, setting fires, provoking the people and chanting slogans that were unrelated to the rationing issue or increase in the price of fuel. They use special signs and symbols to identify each other more easily during their operations."

The IRGC's spokesperson, Ramezan Sharif, was quoted by Mehr News Agency as saying: "Rioters belonged to the MEK. The MEK has a darker track record than the monarchists. They have a violent streak. In a recent poll, the MEK has been identified as the most hated group." Mehr News Agency adds: "He pointed to the fact that the rioters were trained, equipped and organized by the MEK in order to plot against the country and said: 'These people carry out tangible activities both in the realm of a soft war and cultural warfare, as well as in the area of inciting insecurity.'" (November 20)

The IRGC-affiliated Javan newspaper wrote: "The manner in which rioters appeared on the scene shows full well that they entered through a communications network and that they were organized, equipped, coordinated, and had a well-defined and secure communications network, and conducted secret maneuvers. They used predetermined codes." (November 19)

Khamenei's representative in Gilan Province, Rasoul Falahati, said: "We know that you (protesters) are the children of the executed MEK members. You are the children of the MEK in exile. ... We know who you are. ... You should no longer walk the same path as your ill-fated predecessors. You should come back to the arms of the people. Repent! The Judiciary must firmly hand down the ultimate punishment

> *Jomhouri Eslami* **daily: "The scale of the destruction was so vast and the actions were carried out so professionally that it was obvious that a well-trained and well-equipped network was at work, which had financial and strong intelligence support."**

for the main elements of the recent riots. They are responsible for disturbing the peace." (Baran TV, November 20)

The state-run Afkar News said on November 20: "The detainees are in some shape or form tied to the MEK and foreign elements. They received the necessary training over the last two years in order to carry out these actions."

> **Khamenei's representative in Gilan Province, Rasoul Falahati: "We know that you (protesters) are the children of the executed MEK members. You are the children of the MEK in exile."**

The IRGC-affiliated *Javan* newspaper wrote in an editorial by its editor Abdollah Ganji: "Attacks conducted against sensitive centers, including military and law enforcement centers, marked the unique feature of this episode. Attacks were carried out against dozens of police stations, IRGC and Bassij centers, using cold weapons and firearms. Several Bassij members were surrounded and killed. Therefore, the core of the attacks shows the extent of violence and coordination of the riot. ... Special roles were defined for women. They played a fundamental role both in attacking our Bassij sisters and evoking emotions among the youth. Although they did not have any casualties, the manner in which women were employed is similar to the maneuvers of women in the MEK." (November 20)

Ali Shamkhani, Secretary for the Supreme National Security Council: "I believe 34 MEK members have been arrested so far. A vast network of individuals, operating not under the MEK's name, but pursuing their line and modus operandi, were also identified." (Defa' Press, November 24)

Protesters set a billboard with images of Khomeini and Khamenei on fire during the November 2019 uprising.

Ebrahim Raisi, the Judiciary Chief: "The same people, who exploited the public's state of anxiety and demands in order to incite riots and insecurity, and their masters should know that severe punishment awaits them." (Mizan News Agency – November 21)

Alireza Adyani, head of the Ideological-political Organization of the police force: "The incidents of recent days in the country were more complicated than those which occurred in 1999, 2009 and 2018. In one day alone, unrest erupted in 165 cities of 25 provinces. The recent sedition caused insecurity in 900 locations..." (Rasa News Agency, November 21)

> **Alireza Adyani, head of the Ideological-political Organization of the police force: "In one day alone, unrest erupted in 165 cities of 25 provinces."**

> "I believe 34 MEK members have been arrested so far. A vast network of individuals, operating not under the MEK's name, but pursuing their line and modus operandi, were also identified."

Salar Abnoush, Commander of Bassij Operations: "There was an all-out world war against the state and the revolution. A strange and incredible coordination in the current sedition was formed and they were only waiting for a spark to destroy the country. Additional information will be provided after extracting confessions… I believe God was our savior." (ISNA News Agency, November 21)

Gholamhossein Esmaili, the Judiciary Spokesman: "According to the IRGC's report, around 100 leaders and essential elements of these riots have been arrested in different parts of the country. Other people, more than the above, have been identified by the MOIS and a number of them have been arrested, or are on the verge of being arrested." (*Javan* weekly, November 24)

Chapter 3
Suppression and the regime's crimes

Overview

The regime's Assembly of Experts issued a statement on November 22, calling on "all security and judiciary organs to identify, confront, and put on trial the leaders and elements responsible for the riots, and to deal with them with unqualified decisiveness."

On November 21, Tehran Radio broadcast a speech by Tehran's Friday prayer leader Ahmad Khatami. He told his audience: "One of the expectations from you is to identify the thugs. ... Without any feelings of empathy, report these thugs to officials. Do the same thing that you did against the *hypocrites* (MEK) in the first stage of the revolution. You saw how we got rid of the MEK. People came on the scene. Sometimes, a father whose son was an MEK supporter would turn him in. I believe that in view of the extensive plot that these people designed, we must seek and pursue them from house to house and turn them in to officials."

UPRISING SHAKES IRAN REGIME'S FOUNDATIONS

Protesters gather to confront state security forces in the southern city of Shiraz.

Khatami added: "I say to the Judiciary: The first thing is that judicial officials must hand down the ultimate punishment to the organizers and leaders of these gangs, those who killed people, those who committed robbery, those who intimidated, whether it was they, themselves or they cooperated with others. As a cleric with over 20 years of experience teaching in religious seminaries about *fiqh* (Islamic jurisprudence), I say that these people are *baqi* (disobedient), they are *mohareb* (waging war on God), and they must face the ultimate punishment (i.e. death). Regarding their followers, I say to the Judiciary that you must act with decisiveness so that these people would forever feel remorseful and never feel the urge to commit such riots again. And, others would learn a lesson about this episode."

On November 21, the state-run Baran TV broadcast a speech by Mullah Falahati, the Friday prayer leader in the northern city of Rasht, who said: "The Judiciary must firmly hand down the ultimate punishment for the main elements of the recent riots who are responsible for disturbing the peace."

> **Tehran's Friday prayer leader Ahmad Khatami: "… judicial officials must hand down the ultimate punishment to the organizers and leaders of these gangs."**

The regime's prosecutor in Alborz Province, Haji Reza Shakarami, said: "The judge can declare that those who disrupt security, if they intend to overthrow the system or damage public and private assets, are *mohareb* or *mofsid fil-arz* (corrupters of the Earth; both charges carry death sentences). They themselves are responsible for the consequences." (*Serat News*, November 19)

The state-run *Kayhan* daily wrote on November 19: "Some of the reports indicate that judicial officials are certain that punishment by the noose will be delivered to the leaders of the recent riots."

> **The state-run *Kayhan*: "…judicial officials are certain that punishment by the noose will be delivered to the leaders of the recent riots."**

Red alert mobilization and organizational chart

Organizational structure of the regime's apparatus of suppression during an uprising (State of emergency and red alert)

The clerical regime declared a red alert during the uprising, in accordance with which, starting at 1400 local time on Saturday, November 16, 2019, the Islamic Revolutionary Guard Corps (IRGC) completely took command of the nationwide suppression and all suppressive forces. This report provides a summary of the organizational structure of the suppression. (See the Command chart in the next section.)

1. **Preparation of the suppression machinery prior to the announcement of the fuel price hike:** From November 10, the regime's suppressive apparatus, including the IRGC, the State Security Forces (SSF), the Ministry of Intelligence and Security (MOIS), and the Sarollah Garrison, were put on alert. In addition to meetings held by the Supreme National Security Council, the Interior Ministry's Security Council chaired by Brig. Gen. Hossein Zolfaqari was established and various security plans were reviewed in the provinces across the country. Zolfaqari is the deputy security and law enforcement official in the Interior Ministry. In these meetings, the MOIS was represented by Mirshafiei, a deputy minister. Brig. Gen. Mohammad Kazemi, head of the Protection section of the IRGC Intelligence Organization and a representative of the IRGC Sarollah Garrison, were also present. It was declared in these meetings that the decision to increase fuel prices was considered top secret and that all actions must be taken in accordance with orders and the regime's plan.

    It is noteworthy that the Security Council of the Interior Ministry and the Provincial Council controlled security matters before the emergency declaration and red alert. After the declaration was made, the IRGC took direct command over the suppression, with all other security organs, including the SSF and the MOIS, taking their orders from the IRGC.

2. **Khamenei's role at the helm of the suppression:** The dictatorship's top authority, Ali Khamenei, personally oversaw the suppression. On Sunday morning, November 17, he publicly endorsed the decision to hike fuel prices and acknowledged that he was behind the announcement. He also issued an order to suppress the protests. The brutal wave of suppression subsequently intensified, with IRGC snipers and forces targeting the protesters' heads and chests in a bid to slaughter them.

3. **The regime's Supreme National Security Council:** This council is chaired by the regime's president, Hassan Rouhani, and is the highest decision-making body in the country when it comes to political and security matters. The heads of the three branches of government are all permanent members of the council, which signed the order to increase fuel prices. All the members were also involved in the suppression of the uprising.

4. **IRGC Supreme Command Council:** Chaired by the IRGC Commander-in-Chief, this body is comprised of all the IRGC senior commanders. It is the highest decision-making body in the IRGC and oversees suppression in Iran. After unrest erupted in Iran in 2009, the regime recognized the potential

for an uprising as its most existential threat. The IRGC was consequently reorganized in 2009 and divided into provincial divisions for each of the 31 provinces. During the November 2019 uprising, the IRGC established itself as critically and criminally key to the brutal suppression.

5. **Sarollah Garrison, Command HQ of Suppression in Tehran Province:** In view of the sensitive status of the capital city, Tehran, for the dictatorship's existence, the clerical regime established a concentrated suppression garrison named Sarollah. The IRGC Commander-in-Chief is the commander of this base, which commands all of the regime's other suppressive organs, including the SSF and the MOIS, during a state of emergency. Sarollah Garrison has divided Tehran Province into four regions for suppression. (See the organizational chart attached.)

6. **Provincial IRGC command bases:** In each province, the province's IRGC Commander oversees the operations of all suppressive forces. In a state of emergency, the SSF, MOIS provincial office, the local judiciary and other organs are under the command of the provincial IRGC, similar to the Sarollah Garrison model instituted in Tehran.

Clearly, the organizational structure of the suppression of the Iranian people's uprising has the person of Khamenei at the helm, with the IRGC playing a command role. Despite the comprehensive preparations that all of the regime's suppressive forces had made, they could not control the uprising after it started. They, therefore, quickly declared a red alert in the entire country, cut off the Internet, and resorted to a massacre as ordered by Khamenei and the IRGC's command.

> **Despite the comprehensive preparations that all of the regime's suppressive forces had made, they could not control the uprising after it started. They, therefore, quickly declared a red alert in the entire country, cut off the Internet, and resorted to a massacre as ordered by Khamenei and the IRGC's command.**

Command chart of regime's apparatus of suppression during an uprising (State of emergency and red alert)

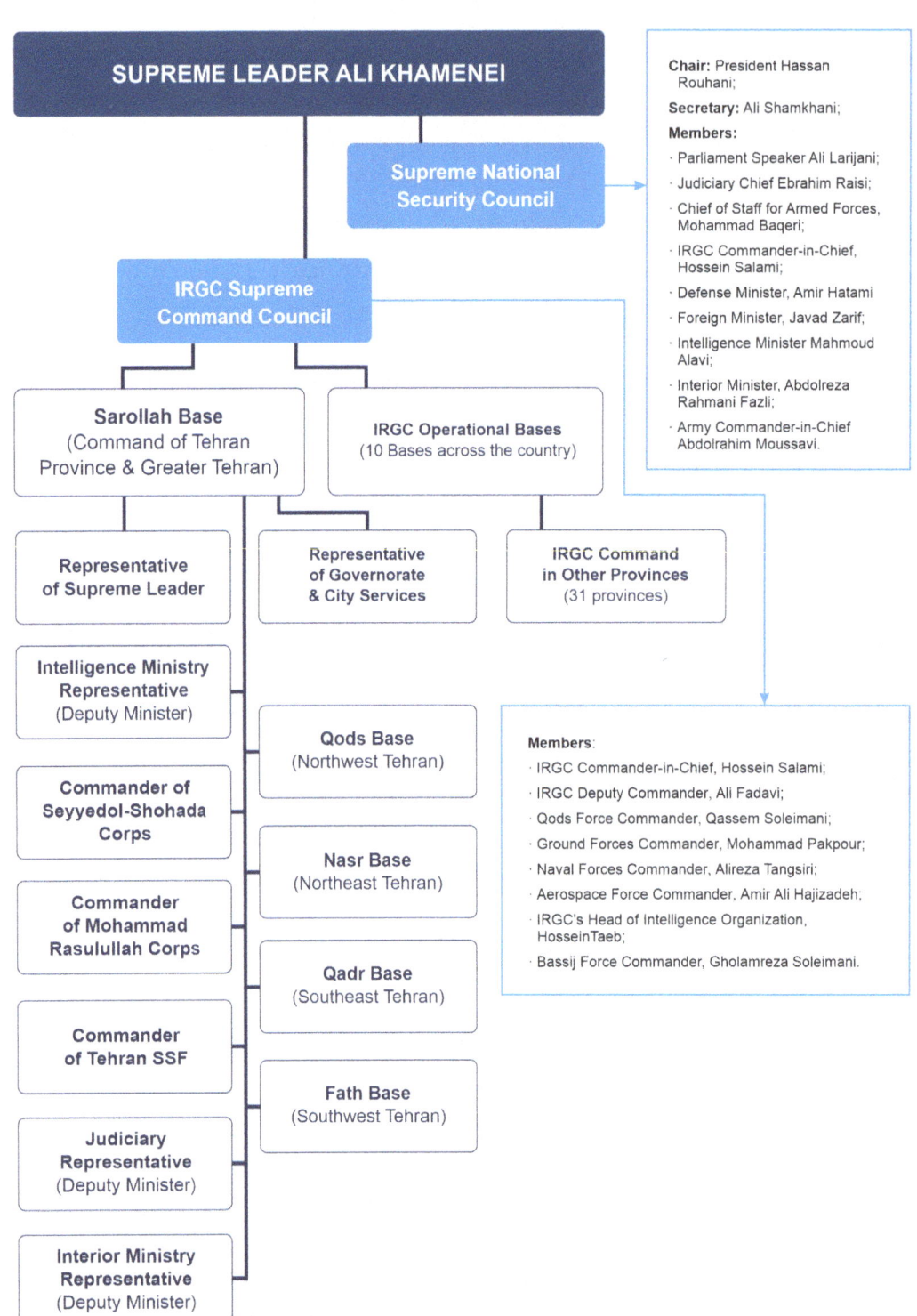

"Controlling Riots and Protests"

In a highly confidential directive, entitled "Controlling Riots and Protests," the operational methods to crack down on popular protests have been outlined. Obtained from the "Law Enforcement Force of the Islamic Republic of Iran" (Farsi acronym NAJA, referred to as State Security Force, SSF, in this report), the directive lists the SSF's suppressive modus operandi and definitions.

According to information obtained by the MEK from within the regime, at 2:00 pm local time, Saturday, November 16, the SSF declared a state of red alert, whereby the SSF handed over responsibility for suppression of the uprising to the Islamic Revolutionary Guards Corps (IRGC). SSF forces were put under IRGC command, making it palpably clear that the SSF was unable to control the situation and the regime felt itself in critical danger.

An alert regarding the state of the nation's security is defined as:
1. Normal state: White
2. Abnormal state: Gray
3. Extraordinary state: Yellow
4. Critical state: Red

Demonstrators challenge state security forces under a cloud of smoke.

> **SSF forces were put under IRGC command, making it palpably clear that the SSF was unable to control the situation and the regime felt itself in critical danger.**

Red alert

The regime's definition: "In this critical situation, the country's vital locations and facilities, military, law enforcement, and intelligence centers come under attack and are occupied. In these circumstances,

1. If this happens in a city or a province, the IRGC with all available forces enters into action if necessary, on the orders of the commander-in-chief of the armed forces or the Supreme National Security Council.

2. The SSF is placed under the IRGC's operational control and carries out its responsibilities.

3. The Ministry of Intelligence and the Judiciary provide the necessary logistical support.

4. All government organizations and institutions are duty-bound to put their resources, based on the statement by the Supreme National Security Council, at the disposal of the region's senior military commander to support the actions of the SSF.

5. If this situation expands to several provinces or throughout the country, the SNSC will take more decisions that are fundamental."

Command and Control Headquarters

Another directive, also obtained from the SSF, entitled "Operational Actions of the Command and Control HQ," outlines comprehensive and detailed planning for suppression of popular protests. It is classified as "Highly Confidential."

The pamphlet characterizes and divides protests into three alert status:

- Operational action by the command and control headquarters vis-à-vis peaceful but unlawful assemblies (Status 1)
- Operational action by the command and control headquarters vis-à-vis unlawful assemblies during police action (Status 2)
- Operational action by the command and control headquarters vis-à-vis general rebellion (Status 3)

According to the above status definitions, the recent uprising of the Iranian people is status 3. The pamphlet outlines some actions related to this status:

Internal Actions

- Issue alert to provinces and activate second battle order
- Issue order to special unit to dispatch forces to the relevant provincial center
- Video monitoring of the mission location

External Actions

- Notification to provincial prosecutor
- Notification to provincial IRGC and request dispatch of reinforcements
- Notification to provincial Intelligence [MOIS]

Translation of Original Document: "Actions of Provincial Command and Control Headquarters"

Internal Organizational Actions

1. Immediate notification to SSF Operations Directorate at CCHQ (Command and Control Headquarters)

2. Notification to chain of command
3. Issue alert to provinces and activate second battle order
4. Notification to heads of special police (prevention, investigations, intelligence and security)
5. Issue order to special unit to dispatch forces to the relevant provincial center
6. Dispatch of reinforcements from other provincial centers
7. Request reinforcements from SSF CCHQ if necessary
8. Issue alert to provincial investigative and neutralization team and dispatch to scene of incident if necessary
9. Video monitoring of the mission location
10. Notification to provincial border control (for border provinces)
11. Notification to provincial social directorate to document and coordinate with press for publication of news to prevent rumors
12. Notification to provincial social directorate to conduct interviews in accordance with the commander's aims and instructions and notifications issued from the Supreme National Security Council
13. Issue order to provincial centers to increase protection of officials and classified facilities
14. Issue alert orders to neighboring provincial centers
15. Issue alert to medical services to send special ambulances for your own forces
16. Dispatch special investigative unit of provincial operations directorate to scene of incident.
17. Notify SSF CCHQ of updates
18. Request SSF announce alert
19. Implement plan to recall personnel in neighboring provincial centers (if necessary)
20. Implement plan to recall personnel (if necessary)

External Organizational Actions

1. Notification to provincial governor and follow up for convening of provincial protection council

اقدامات مرکز فرماندهی و کنترل استان

اقدامات درون سازمانی:

1- اطلاع‌رسانی آنی به مرفوک معاونت عملیات ناجا
2- اطلاع‌رسانی به سلسله مراتب فرماندهی
3- اعلام آمادگی به شهرستان‌ها و فعال نمودن سازمان دوم رزم
4- اطلاع‌رسانی به روسای پلیس های تخصصی (پیشگیری، آگاهی و پاوا)
5- ابلاغ به یگان ویژه برای اعزام نیرو به شهرستان مربوطه
6- اعزام نیروهای کمکی از سایر شهرستان‌ها
7- درخواست نیروی کمکی از مرفوک ناجا در صورت لزوم
8- اعلام آمادگی به تیم کشف و خنثی سازی استان و در صورت لزوم، اعزام به محل حادثه
9- پایش تصویری محل ماموریت
10- اطلاع‌رسانی به مرزبانی استان (برای استان های مرزی)
11- اعلام به معاونت اجتماعی استان جهت مستندسازی و هماهنگی با رسانه ها جهت انتشار اخبار مربوطه به منظور جلوگیری از شایعه پراکنی
12- ابلاغ به معاونت اجتماعی استان برای انجام مصاحبه بنا به تدبیر فرمانده و دستورالعمل های ابلاغی اطلاع‌رسانی صادره از شاک
13- ابلاغ به شهرستان‌ها جهت تشدید حفاظت از مسئولین و اماکن دارای طبقه بندی
14- صدور دستورات هوشیاری به شهرستان های همجوار
15- اعلام به بهداری برای اعزام آمبولانس ویژه نیروهای خودی
16- اعزام تیم کارشناسی معاونت عملیات استان به محل برای بررسی
17- اعلام اخبار تکمیلی به مرکز فرماندهی و کنترل ناجا
18- درخواست از ناجا برای اعلام آماده باش
19- اجرای طرح احضار برای شهرستان های همجوار (در صورت لزوم)
20- اجرای طرح احضار پرسنل (در صورت لزوم)

اقدامات برون سازمانی:

1- اعلام به استاندار و پیگیری جهت تشکیل شورای تامین استان
2- اعلام به مرکز اورژانس استان جهت اعزام آمبولانس و انتقال مصدومین به مراکز درمانی در صورت لزوم
3- هماهنگی با بیمارستان های استان درصورت اعزام مصدومان تجمع به خارج از شهرستان
4- اعلام به دادستان استان
5- اطلاع به سپاه استان و اعلام آمادگی برای اعزام نیرو در صورت ضرورت
6- اعلام به اطلاعات استان

The Farsi original "Actions of Provincial Command and Control Headquarters" directive

2. Notification to provincial emergency center to send ambulances and transport injured to medical centers if necessary
3. Coordination with provincial hospitals in case of transfer of injured from assemblies to outside of the province
4. Notification to provincial prosecutor
5. Notification to provincial IRGC and request for dispatch of reinforcements
6. Notification to provincial Intelligence [MOIS]

Wireless communications reveal regime's inability to curb protests

Intercepted wireless communications between repressive security forces in the city of Robat Karim and IRGC Brigadier General Hossein Rahimi, head of the Greater Tehran Security Zone, on November 16 indicate the growing fear among the commanders on the ground. The voice of the security commander reporting from the Governorate office is heard requesting immediate reinforcements: "The situation is red. The protesters are heading towards the Governorate office. They are around

> "The situation is red. The protesters are heading towards the Governorate office. They are around 5,000 people. If Bashir [garrison forces] comes late, the Governorate will fall."

5,000 people. If Bashir [garrison forces] comes late, the Governorate will fall. The transcript of the communication:

- Command Post to Bashir: Tell Bashir-2 to report to Robat Karim's Governorate
- Copy that.
- Ammar1 HQ: Go ahead
- The situation is red. The protesters are heading towards the Governorate office. They are around 5000 people. If Bashir comes late, the Governorate will fall.
- Anvari: Get help from IRGC elements close by. I will speak with Bashir as well.
- Bashir-2 from HQ: IRGC says they have no orders. They will not help. They recommend using plainclothes agents.
- Plainclothes won't do the job.
- Coordination was arranged whereby the IRGC would come to your aid from their garrison out there and protect the Governorate. Why won't they come?
- They say they have no such orders. I can't do the job with only plainclothes. They are destroying everything. There are 5000 people.

Wireless communications of suppressive forces in Shahriar district, southwest Tehran, recorded by Resistance units

The following communication indicates that the special reinforcement unit of the State Security Force, assigned to suppress protest gatherings, was forced to retreat by protesters.

- Command Center: Has the reinforcement unit arrived yet?
- Reply: The unit is here but they are being forced to retreat.
- Headquarters: OK, it will be relayed to colleagues at the headquarters

UPRISING SHAKES IRAN REGIME'S FOUNDATIONS

A communication about capture of a police station and a center of the paramilitary Bassij force

- From headquarters to Malek-1: What is the priority now, Vali-Asr or Faz-1? (two areas in Shahriar). Relay this message to Malek, relay to Malek, relay to Malek-1 and ask if Faz-1 is the priority now or not. If you have no problem in Vali-Asr, dispatch forces of Heydar, Malek-1 also go to Faz-1 and wrap up the problem there.
- Police Command Center: My friends, please note, Rahvar (Traffic Police) base in Saba-Shahr (suburb of Shahriar) has been overrun and the Bassij base of Mireh has also been overrun. According to 21-1 (code name of a police unit), they are now moving toward Saba-Shahr.

Massacre in Mahshahr

According to numerous reports, the mullahs' regime carried out a vicious killing spree, a massacre, on November 18 against protesters in Mahshahr, a southwestern city with a population of 120,000 people. In a December 2 frontpage article entitled "As Angry Citizens Staged Protests, Iran Opened Fire," *The New York Times* cited eyewitness reports, writing that in Mahshahr alone, witnesses and emergency officials said 40 to 100 civilians were killed by the Revolutionary Guards (IRGC), many of them young.

"Security forces began firing into the marshes at around 10:30 am on Monday, November 18," one eyewitness said. "The security forces opened fire into the marshes once again on Monday night."

The following is an exclusive report provided by Mahshahr residents:

"The IRGC units stationed in Khuzestan Province dispatched a commando brigade to Mahshahr under orders from the Khuzestan governor after locals blocked a road leading to nearby petrochemical sites. The units were equipped with tanks, armored personnel carriers, a variety of heavy and semi-heavy weaponry, and

A screen shot of a clip showing SSF trucks equipped with machine guns in the marshes of Mahshahr, November 18, 2019

even military gunships. These units first entered the Chamran (Jarahi) district and began opening fire on the people using AK-47s and 50-caliber heavy machine guns. They were also opening fire on civilians from helicopters. They were even targeting those in their homes who had not participated in the protests. Around 17 individuals, including two 4 and 8-year-old children, and even an old woman above the age of 70, were killed from direct IRGC fire." (The exact number of those killed remains uncertain due to the fact that the youth were seen fleeing to the marshes and the IRGC opened fire blindly into the wetlands.)

> **"These units first entered the Chamran (Jarahi) district and began opening fire on the people using AK-47s and 50-caliber heavy machine guns. They were also opening fire on civilians from helicopters."**

UPRISING SHAKES IRAN REGIME'S FOUNDATIONS

On Monday, December 2, a resident of Mahshahr said: "I'm from this city and you know that in the recent protests we had the highest number of protesters killed after Kermanshah (western Iran). With over 20 petrochemical sites, Mahshahr is one of the largest petrochemical hubs in Iran and even in the Middle East. Bandar Khomeini, which is one of Iran's largest commercial ports, is also located here. It is also one of the country's largest oil exporting ports. (Most of Iran's oil and the Abadan oil refineries' production are exported through Mahshahr and Khark.) More significantly, Mahshahr is located between the two rivers of Zohreh and Jarahi. As a result, it has a very special agricultural and fishing stature among the cities of Khuzestan Province.

"The largest storage tanks and export sites of gasoline, diesel fuel, other oil products and various goods are near Mahshahr. While this city is the second largest in Khuzestan Province after Ahvaz, the locals of Mahshahr are living in utter poverty. Unemployment and poverty are rampant in many areas of Mahshahr…

"The IRGC even ordered the city hospital to refuse medical care to those injured in these clashes. The IRGC units entered three other districts on that same day where they continued their killing sprees. Clashes continued in the Taleghani district, where locals are armed. They defended themselves and heavy gunfire continued non-stop from 6 pm Tuesday (November 19) to 1 am Wednesday (November 20). They entered the area with tanks, yet the locals defended their homes. The IRGC also suffered many casualties. Local sheikhs and elders mediated, resulting in an end to the clashes and the Taleghani district was surrounded. For three days the IRGC and other security forces were arresting youths in these areas. Clashes have stopped but the situation remains tense."

Mahshahr police chief Reza Papi claimed members of dissident groups had sought refuge in the marshes and from there opened fire on his units. Mahshahr Governor Mohsen Biranvand said in a state TV interview that the main imports from the port of Mahshahr were being threatened, and considering the fact that only 400 trucks are delivering goods into the country each day from this port, it was vital for security forces to take urgent action.

Chapter 4
Regime officials involved in suppression of the uprising

Introduction

In this report, the Iranian Resistance has for the first time exposed details and photos of 92 of the key officials involved in the senseless, extrajudicial, and violent repression, murder, wounding, and detention of protesters in the seven provinces of Tehran, Alborz, Khuzestan, Fars, Isfahan, Kurdistan, and Kermanshah. These provinces were the scenes of the most significant, widespread, and pervasive of the recent protests.

UPRISING SHAKES IRAN REGIME'S FOUNDATIONS

Who's in charge?

Ali Khamenei
Regime's Supreme Leader

Hassan Rouhani
Regime's President

Mullah Ebrahim Raisi
Chief Justice

Ali Shamkhani
Secretary of SNSC

Hossein Salami
Commander-in-chief of IRGC

Qassem Soleimani
Commander of the Qods Force

Mohammad Pakpour
Ground Forces Commander of IRGC

UPRISING SHAKES IRAN REGIME'S FOUNDATIONS

IRGC Brig Gen. Hossein Ashtari
Commander of SSF

Gholamreza Soleimani
Commander of Bassij Force

Mullah Hossein Taeb
Head of IRGC Intelligence Org

Mullah Mahmoud Alavi
Intelligence Minister

Mohammad-Javad Azari Jahromi
Minister of Information and Communications Technology

Alireza Avayi
Justice Minister

Ali Fadavi
Deputy Chief of IRGC

Abdolreza Rahmani Fazli
Interior Minister

Tehran Province

The capital Tehran, and other cities in Tehran Province were centers of protest from November 15 to 23. During this period, Tehran state security forces killed at least 83 protesters and wounded up to 800.

Some of the Iranian regime's officials involved in the criminal killing, wounding, and arrest of protesters:

IRGC of Greater Tehran
Mohammad Rasoulollah Corps

Mohammad-Reza Yazdi
Commander of Mohammad Rasoulollah Corps

Sirous Saberi
Deputy Commander of Mohammad Rasoulollah Corps

Hossein Dini
Deputy Coordinator of Mohammad Rasoulollah Corps

Mohammad Na'imi
representative of the Supreme Leader in Mohammad Rasoulollah Corps

Tehran Province Security Council

Mohammad Esmail Kosari
Deputy Commander of Sarollah Base of IRGC in Tehran

Hossein Salami
Commander in Chief of the IRCG and Commander of Sarollah Base of IRGC in Tehran

Anoushirvan Mohseni Band-Pey
Governor

Hamid Reza Goudarzi
Governor's Deputy on Security and Police Affairs

Ali Alqasi Mehr
Revolutionary Prosecutor General

Director General of Intelligence in Tehran Province

Hossein Rahimi
Commander of SSF of Greater Tehran

Kiomars Azizi
Commander of SSF in east of province

Mohsen Khancherli
Commander of SSF in west of province

Hassan Hassan-Zadeh
Commander of Seyyed Alshohada Corps in Tehran Province

Mohammad-Reza Yazdi
Commander of Mohammad Rasoulollah Corps of Greater Tehran

IRGC of Tehran Province
Seyyed Alshohada Corp

Hassan Hassan-Zadeh
Commander of Seyyed Alshohada Corps in Tehran Province

Colonel Alireza Heydarnia
Deputy Coordinator of Seyyed Alshohada Corps

Colonel Majid Amir Abdullahian
Deputy Coordinator of Seyyed Alshohada Corps

Kurdistan Province

Two cities in Kurdistan Province, Sanandaj and Marivan, were among the epicenters of the uprising from November 15 to 23. The Iranian regime's security forces killed fifty-three protesters and wounded about 500 during the course of the first few days of unrest.

Officials responsible for the killing, wounding, and arrest of the protesters include:

Command of Kurdistan Province's Islamic Revolutionary Guards Corps (IRGC) – Beit ol-Moqaddas Corps

Brig. Gen. Seyed Sadeq Hosseini
Beit ol-Moqaddas Corps Commander

Brig. Gen. Hamzeh Fallah,
Beit ol-Moqaddas Corps Deputy Commander

Col. Jamshid Azadipor
Beit ol-Moqaddas Corps Deputy Coordinator

Ahmad Jalili
Khamenei's Rep. in Beit ol-Moqaddas Corps

Kurdistan Provincial Security Council

Hossein Khosh-Eghbal
Security and Social Political Deputy

Bahman Moradnia
Governor

Mohammad Jabbari
Revolutionary Prosecutor General

Ali Azadi
Commander of State Security Forces of Kurdistan Province

Brig. Gen. Seyed Sadeq Hosseini
Beit ol-Moqaddas Corps Commander

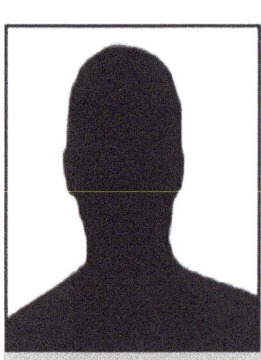
Provincial Intelligence Director General

Marivan

Col. Vali Aei
Marivan IRGC Commander

Khuzestan Province

Two cities in Khuzestan Province, Ahwaz and Mahshahr were in revolt November 14 to 23. During this period, security forces killed 87 protesters and wounded nearly 900 in the province.

Criminals implicated in the killing, wounding, and arrest of protesters in Khuzestan include:

IRGC Command Khuzestan Province (Hazrat-e-vali-Asr Corps)

General Hassan Shahvarpoor
Hazrat-e-vali-Asr Corps
Commander

Colonel Abdolreza Hajati
Coordinator and Deputy Commander
Hazrat-e-vali-Asr Corps

General Moinpoor
Second-in-command
Hazrat-e-vali-Asr Corps

Mullah Abdolreza Rastegari
Khamenei's representative
Hazrat-e-vali-Asr Corps

Abadan
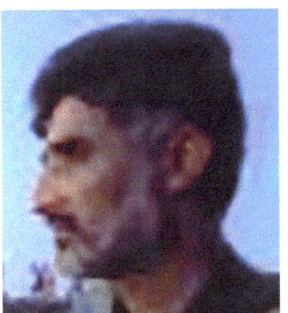
IRGC Lt. Colonel Ahmadi
IRGC Commander for Abadan

Andimeshk

IRGC Lt. Colonel Abollah Kheiranpoor
IRGC Commander for Behbahan district

Behbahan

IRGC Lt. Colonel Ehsan Karimpoor
IRGC Commander for Andimeshk

Mahshahr

IRGC Colonel Karim Babaei
IRGC Commander for Mahshahr

Khuzestan Province Security Council

Habibollah Asefi
Deputy for Security

Gholamreza Shariati
Governor

Abbas Hosseini Pooya
Revolutionary Prosecutor general

Ali-Hossein Hosseinzadeh
Social-political deputy

Heydar Abbaszadeh
State security forces' commander

Hassan Shahvarpoor
Commander IRGC Vali-e-Asr provincial Corps

Hossein Bagherzadeh
Intelligence Director-general for the province

Mahshahr City Security Council

IRGC Colonel Karim Babaei
IRGC Commander for Mahshahr

Mohsen Biravand
Governor of Mahshahr

IRGC Colonel Reza Papi
SSF Commander for Mahshahr

Mehdi Mohammadi
Revolutionary Prosecutor General for Mahshahr

Kermanshah Province

Two of the main centers of revolt in Kermanshah Province, November 14-22, were the cities of Kermanshah and Javanrood.

Some of the criminals who took part in killing, injuring, and arresting protesters are:

IRGC Command Kermanshah province (Nabi Akram Corps)

General Bahman Rohani
Commander of Nabi Akram Corps

Colonel Morteza Moradi
Second-in-command of Nabi Akram Corps

Mullah Shamsollah Jalilian
Khamenei's representative in Nabi Akram Corps

Colonel Bayati
Deputy Coordinator for Nabi Akram Corps

Colonel Moussavi
Inspector General of Nabi Akram Corps

Kermansheh Province Security Council

Mohamad-Ebrahim Elahi-Tabar
Political-security and social deputy

Hooshang Bazvand
Governor

Mohamad-Hossein Sadeghi
Revolutionary Prosecutor general

Ali-Akbar Javidan
State security forces's commander

Bahman Reyhani
Commander
IRGC Nabi Akram provincial Corps

Haji Khorassani
Intelligence Director-general for the province

Javanrood

IRGC Lt. Colonel Abouzar Anvari
Commander of Javanrood Coprs

Fars Province

Shiraz and Kazeroun in Fars Province formed major centers of uprising from November 15 to November 23. During this period, regime security forces martyred 30 of the protesters and wounded some 300.

Criminals directly involved in murdering, injuring, and arresting protesters include:

Command of the IRGC in Fars Province (Fajr Corps)

Brigadier Hashem Ghlasl
Commander of Fajr Corps

Brigadier Yadollah Bouali
Deputy Commander of Fajr Corps

**IRGC Colonel
Ali Mohammad Mohammadi**
Deputy Coordinator of Fajr Corps

Fars Province Security Council

Seyed Ahmad Ahmadizadeh
Deputy Governor for Political, Security, Social Affairs

Enayat'ollah Rahimi
Governor

Heydar Asiyabi
Revolutionary Prosecutor General

Rahambakhsh Habibi
Commander of State Security Forces of Fars Province

Brigadier Hashem Ghiasi
Commander of IRGC Fajr Corps (assigned to Fars Province)

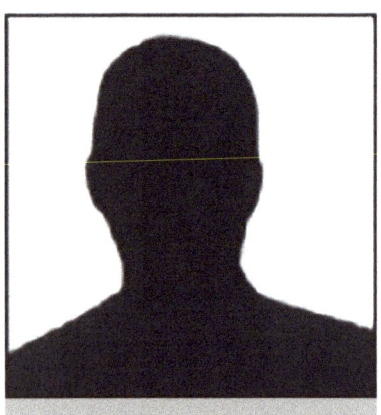

Director of the MOIS in Fars Province

Kazeroun

IRGC Lt. Colonel Shahram Afshari
Commander of IRGC in Kazeroun

Isfahan Province

One of the main areas of uprising from November 15 to 23 was Isfahan and its suburbs. During this period, 32 of the protesters were martyred and some 300 were wounded.

The murderers who were directly involved in killing, injuring, and arresting protesters include:

Command of the IRGC in Isfahan Province

Brigadier Mojtaba Fada
Commander of IRGC in Isfahan Province

Colonel Abedini
Deputy Coordinator of IRGC in Isfahan

Isfahan Province Security Council

Heydar Ghasemi
Deputy Governor for Political, Security, Social Affairs

Abbas Rezaie
Governor

Ali Esfahani
Revolutionary Prosecutor General

Mehdi Masoumbeygi
Commander of State Security Forces of Isfahan Province

IRGC Brigadier Mojtaba Fada
Commander of IRGC Sahebol Zaman Corps (assigned to Isfahan Province)

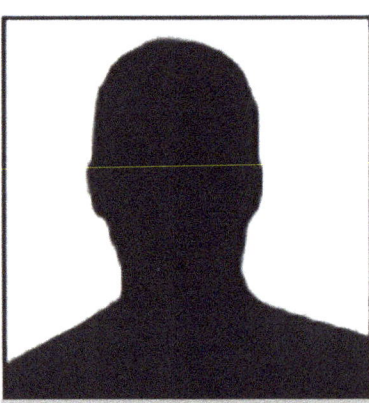

Bahrami
Director of the MOIS in Isfahan Province

Alborz Province

Karaj city was one of the most active centers of uprisings from November 15 to 23, along with other towns and cities in this province. During this period, state security forces killed 9 protesters and arrested about 100 in this province.

Key criminal officials involved in killing, wounding, and arrest of protesters are as follows:

IRGC Brigadier General Yousef Molaie
Commander of Imam Hassan Mojtaba Corps

Ali Tarkashvand
Head of Bassij Construction Organization of Imam Hassan Mojtaba Corps

IRGC Colonel Valiollah Shadman
Deputy Coordinator of Imam Hassan Mojtaba Corps

Mullah Alimorad Yousefi
Supreme Leader's Representative in Imam Hassan Mojtaba Corps

Alborz Province Security Council

Unidentified

Azizollah Shahbazi
Governor

Haji Reza Shah Karami
Revolutionary Prosecutor General

Abbas-Ali Mohammadian
Commander of State Security Forces in Alborz Province

IRGC Brigadier General Yousef Molaie
Commander of Imam Hassan Mojtaba Corps

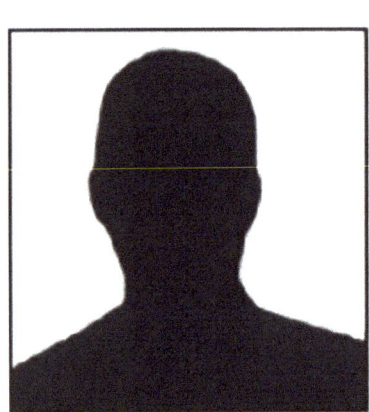
General Director of the MOIS in Alborz Province

Chapter 5
Main takeaways of the November uprising

1. The decision to raise the price of gasoline was a unanimous decision in which the regime in its entirety, including the heads of its three branches as well as all of its factions, were involved, with the full approval of the Supreme Leader, Ali Khamenei. Imposing so extreme a price hike at the expense of the Iranian people reveals the regime's extreme need and desperation.

2. The speed with which the protests expanded to various towns and cities, all with common political slogans that defied the regime in its entirety, revealed the potential and readiness of Iranian society to overthrow the regime.

3. As regime analysts themselves have admitted, contrary to previous protests, this uprising's slogans did not express any demands from the regime. The atmosphere and behavior prevalent among the protesters had radicalized in the extreme. This was demonstrated in the torching of the regime's centers and posters of Khamenei, among other acts. During the 2017-2018 uprising,

UPRISING SHAKES IRAN REGIME'S FOUNDATIONS

there were only 50 attacks on regime centers. This time, however, even though precise figures are still being compiled, it seems that thousands of regime-affiliated buildings were targeted.

4. The suppressive tactics used in this uprising were not comparable to those employed during the uprisings of 2009 and 2017/2018. The number of martyrs, wounded and detainees of the previous protests combined are a fraction of those in the current uprising.

5. This time, Khamenei himself immediately came to the scene and, while announcing that the regime would not retreat (from the gas price hike), he ordered his forces to suppress the protests. This exposes the regime's complete inability to handle any retreat. It is terrified of being overthrown.

6. The unique feature of this uprising compared to the 2018 protests is that, although the driving force in 2018 was the MEK's Resistance units, at that time they were in their infancy and just beginning their endeavors. This time, Resistance units had spread extensively and had gained vast experience from thousands of prior political and social acts of protest.

7. Another difference was that the uprising erupted just as the regime was being hit with major blows to its meddling in Iraq and Lebanon, which Tehran considers its "strategic depth." In Iraq, in particular, people chanted slogans against Khamenei and IRGC Qods Force Commander Qassem Soleimani.

8. The clerical regime and Khamenei himself are faced with a crisis of overthrow and see their only way out as suppressing the popular will and demands. As such, the standing of those demanding overthrow is more strongly consolidated as the alternative in real political terms and the real balance of power.

9. The regime failed to prevent the outbreak of rebellion. The uprising revealed to the entire world the ruling apparatus' weak and unstable situation.

10. The uprising also revealed that the Iranian people are united and have a single voice when it comes to demanding the overthrow of the regime. The people in Fars, Isfahan, Tehran, and Mashhad speak with one voice and relay the same demands as Kurds in Marivan and Sanandaj, and as Arab-Iranians in

Mahshahr and Ahvaz. Everyone sees that the path to democracy and freedom in Iran goes through the overthrow of the clerical regime.

11. The strategy of "Resistance Units and Rebellious Cities," which the Iranian Resistance's Leader announced several years ago prior to the 2018 uprising, has proven its efficacy and legitimacy. In the aftermath of the 2018 uprising, the Iranian Resistance said that the situation in Iran would never revert to what it had been. The recent uprising provided further proof of the correctness of that assessment.

12. The protests have demonstrated not only the desire of the Iranian people for change, but also confirmed that the firm U.S. policy on Iran, including imposition of sanctions, has not rallied people behind the regime. The protests show that public anger is directed at the regime as solely responsible for their suffering.

Chapter 6
What should be done?

- The slaughter of protesters is a clear case of a crime against humanity. Therefore, the United Nations Security Council, governments and the international community should take urgent action to put an immediate halt to the killings and suppression, and secure the release of those detained.

- These atrocities were carried out away from the watchful eyes of Iranians and the outside world after the clerical regime shut down the internet and cut Iran off from the rest of the world. Therefore, investigative missions must be sent to Iran to evaluate the scope of the crimes and examine the cases of those killed, wounded and/or detained.

- The leaders of the regime, beginning with Supreme Leader Ali Khamenei who, on November 17, gave the green light for the all-out crackdown, and

President Hassan Rouhani, who doubled down on Khamenei's call, must be held accountable for crimes against humanity.

- Silence and inaction vis-à-vis these crimes against humanity not only violate international conventions, laws, and standards, but also embolden the mullahs to continue such atrocities in Iran and the region.

- The United States should sanction Western companies and any other entities that aid the Iranian regime with the sale and provision of services, products, and solutions that enable it to monitor, control, and block internet access by Iranian citizens. In addition, the United States should adopt all measures necessary to diminish and disable the regime's capacity to block internet traffic in Iran.

- The United States should provide safe, secure, and uninterruptible internet access to Iran's people, including the protesters, who seek nothing but a free, democratic and nonnuclear republic.

- It is time for the world to recognize the right of the Iranian people to change the repressive regime and establish a democratic, pluralistic and non-nuclear republic based on separation of religion and state.

Appendix 1: Partial list of those fallen for freedom

UPRISING SHAKES IRAN REGIME'S FOUNDATIONS

Names of 724 murdered protesters (identified as of December 31, 2019)

1. Ardabil – Seyed-Ali Fotohi-Kouhsareh
2. Ardabil – Mahyar Qorbani
3. Ardabil – Arash Vakili
4. Isfahan – Arsham Ebrahimi
5. Isfahan – Pasha Ebrahimi
6. Isfahan – Mohammad Ebrahimi
7. Isfahan – ... Estaki
8. Isfahan – Saeed Asadzadeh
9. Isfahan – ... Arasteh
10. Isfahan – Mohammad Arman
11. Isfahan – Farshid Afarin
12. Isfahan – Hossein Baharloo
13. Isfahan – Saeed Baharloo
14. Isfahan – Majid Baharloo
15. Isfahan – Masoud Baharloo
16. Isfahan – Gholamreza Bahrami
17. Isfahan – Hassan Parvaresh
18. Isfahan – Mohammad Pour-Pirali
19. Isfahan – Amir-Hossein Dadvand
20. Isfahan – ... Rahimi
21. Isfahan – Majid Rezaei
22. Isfahan – Hamid Rezaei
23. Isfahan – Mehdi Sabzi
24. Isfahan – Hamid Sharifi
25. Isfahan – ... Shokrollahi
26. Isfahan – Javad Shiyazi
27. Isfahan – Heydar Shiazi
28. Isfahan – Ali Sadeqi
29. Isfahan – Mohammad Javad Abedi
30. Isfahan – Safar Eidivandi
31. Isfahan – Ahmad Qorbani Dastjerdi
32. Isfahan – ... Karaminia
33. Isfahan – Hossein Karimi-Alvijeh
34. Isfahan – ... Koleini
35. Isfahan – Ali Mokhtari
36. Isfahan – Behzad Moenifar
37. Isfahan – Ebrahim Manssouri
38. Isfahan – Ali Mir-Afzali
39. Isfahan – Yaqoub Najafi Hajipour
40. Isfahan (Najafabad) – Mohammad Amiri
41. Isfahan (Zarrinshahr) – Hassan Pour Pirali
42. Isfahan (Zarrinshahr) – Hossein Pour Pirali
43. Yazdanshahr – Rasoul Amani
44. Yazdanshahr - ... Davoudvand
45. Yazdanshahr – Mohammad(Ahmad) Azimi
46. Yazdanshahr – Sassan Eidivand
47. Karaj-Fardis – Babak Allah-Ejdehak
48. Karaj-Fardis – Mohammad Amin-Allahqoli
49. Karaj-Fardis – Reza Paziresh
50. Karaj-Fardis – Faramarz Poursadi
51. Karaj-Fardis – Pedram Jafari Kamijani
52. Karaj-Fardis – Mahmoud Rahimi
53. Karaj-Fardis – Omid Salehi
54. Karaj-Fardis – Alireza Tayabi Salar
55. Karaj-Fardis – Hamid Qa'emi
56. Karaj-Fardis – Ashur Kalna (Christian)
57. Karaj-Fardis – Milad Mojevard
58. Karaj – Bahram Ehsani
59. Karaj – Maysam Ahmadi
60. Karaj – Rahim Akhavan
61. Karaj – Alireza Azadi
62. Karaj – Mehdi Aghyari
63. Karaj – Karim Baqeri
64. Karaj – Poya Bakhtiari
65. Karaj – Rassoul Bakhtiari
66. Karaj – Sadeq Bakhtiari
67. Karaj – Ali Bakhtiari
68. Karaj – Parsa Badarlou
69. Karaj – Ali Pasha
70. Karaj – Mohsen Talivardi
71. Karaj – Hossein Jamali
72. Karaj – Mohsen Chamanfar
73. Karaj – Ali Hosseini
74. Karaj – Mohammad-Reza Hosseini
75. Karaj – Asqar Heshmatpour
76. Karaj – Mehdi Hamami
77. Karaj – Saeed Hamidi
78. Karaj – Mehdi Hamidi
79. Karaj – Heydari Komail
80. Karaj – Bita Khodadadi
81. Karaj – Ali Khoda-Moradi
82. Karaj – Vahid Damvar
83. Karaj – Milad Darvishi
84. Karaj – Hassan Delfan
85. Karaj – Saeed Derakhshan
86. Karaj – Ali Rahmani
87. Karaj – Reza Rahimi
88. Karaj – Mohsen Rahimi

89. Karaj – Omid Rezai
90. Karaj – Nasser Rezai
91. Karaj – Shahla Rezai-Pour
92. Karaj – Dariush Zibanejad-Mofrad
93. Karaj – Mamoud Soltani
94. Karaj – Amir Shokri
95. Karaj – Ms. Ameneh Shahbazi
96. Karaj – Koroush Sheidani
97. Karaj – Mamoud Sadeqpour
98. Karaj – Morteza Sadeqi Nader
99. Karaj – Mehdi Abbaszadeh
100. Karaj – Abbasi-Amjad Mehdi
101. Karaj – Mohammad-Parsa Azizi-Moqadam
102. Karaj – Morteza Alizadeh
103. Karaj – Farrokh Qafari
104. Karaj – Mahan Faramarzi
105. Karaj – Hossein Qassemi
106. Karaj – Amir-Hossein Kabiri
107. Karaj – Ebrahim Ketabdar
108. Karaj – Mehdi Kloukhi
109. Karaj – Mohammad-Mehdi Karimi
110. Karaj – Farhad Majdam
111. Karaj – Alireza Mohammadzadeh
112. Karaj – Sina Mohammadi
113. Karaj – Maysam Mohammadi
114. Karaj – Maysam Moradi
115. Karaj – Ali Morshedi
116. Karaj – Mehdi Moshtaqi
117. Karaj – Reza Mo'azami Goudarzi
118. Karaj – Shahram Moini
119. Karaj – Ebrahim Mehdipour
120. Karaj – Ms. Mahnaz Mehdizadeh-Nader
121. Karaj – Ms. Azar Mirzapour-Zahabi
122. Karaj – Iraj Mishmast
123. Karaj – Mehdi Naghbani
124. Karaj – Hessam Namavar
125. Karaj – Qasem Nematipour
126. Karaj – Mohammad Reza Nikuvaran
127. Karaj – Sajjad Vatankhah
128. Karaj-Golshahr – Mehdi Taherzadeh
129. Meshkin-Dasht – Aziz Eskandari
130. Mehrshar-Karaj – Reza Khazai
131. Mehrshar-Karaj – Nikta Khazai
132. Mehrshar-Karaj – Hamid Rassouli
133. Mehrshar-Karaj – Milad Alipour-Nouri
134. Mehrshar-Karaj – Jalal Nasrabadi
135. Eivan-Gharb – Sajjad Esmaeeli
136. Tabriz – Ali Hosseini
137. Tabriz – Elahe Rastegar
138. Bukan – Shelir Dadvand
139. Bukan – Hiva Naderi
140. Islamshahr – Ali Ahmadi
141. Islamshahr – Mohsen Jafarpanah
142. Islamshahr – Mohammad-Mehdi Haghgouy
143. Islamshahr – Iman Rassouli
144. Islamshahr – Amir Reza Abdullahi
145. Islamshahr – Kamal Faraji
146. Islamshahr – Hossein Qassemi
147. Islamshahr – Arash Kohzadi
148. Islamshahr – Mohsen Mozafari
149. Islamshahr – Mehdi Valipour
150. Baharestan – Fatima Habibi
151. Baharestan – Mohammad Taheri
152. Baharestan – Gol Agha Nouri
153. Boumehen – Behrooz Fallah
154. Boumehen – Arham Moayd Bakhtiari
155. Tehran – Ali-Akbar Abroutan
156. Tehran – Mostafa (Ali) Abrotan-Lanagran
157. Tehran – Abolfazl Arab
158. Tehran – Ali Ostovan
159. Tehran – Nikta Esfandbani (14 year of Age)
160. Tehran – Esmaeel Alahqoli
161. Tehran – Abdollah Ajarloo
162. Tehran – Abolfazl Azarm
163. Tehran – Hassan Babai
164. Tehran – Sajjad Baqeri
165. Tehran – Khosro Bakhtiari
166. Rasht – ... Boniyadi
167. Tehran – Ali Behboudi
168. Tehran – ... Janpanah
169. Tehran – Maysam Jafari
170. Tehran - Ali Chalak
171. Tehran – Majid Hessabi
172. Tehran – Seyed-Qassem Hosseini
173. Tehran – Heydarian Mohammad
174. Tehran – Ramin Dana
175. Tehran – Yusef Dari
176. Tehran – Ali Dahlir
177. Tehran – Hassan Doost
178. Tehran – Samaneh Zolqadr
179. Tehran – Esmaeel Rezazadeh
180. Tehran – Esmael Rezaei-Pirposhteh

UPRISING SHAKES IRAN REGIME'S FOUNDATIONS

181. Tehran – Yasin (Mujtaba) Ramezan-nejad
182. Tehran – ... Ramazani
183. Tehran – Reza Roshan
184. Tehran – Mehran Zahedi
185. Tehran – Ali Sepehri
186. Tehran – Hamzeh Shahsavand
187. Tehran – Ali Shahsavand
188. Tehran – Moussa Shahsavand
189. Tehran – Pedram Shojaee
190. Tehran – Majid Sheikhi
191. Tehran – Mina Sheikhi
192. Tehran – Ali Shirmohammadi
193. Tehran – Amir-Hossein Sadeqi
194. Tehran – Aria Sadeqi
195. Tehran – Mohammad Safari
196. Tehran – Ms. Golnaz Samsami
197. Tehran – Hossein Taheri
198. Tehran – Seyed-Hamid Taheri
199. Tehran – Esmaeel Arab-Ahmadi
200. Tehran – Amir Alizadeh
201. Tehran – Yashar Alizadeh
202. Tehran – Taqi Ali-Loo
203. Tehran – Hossein Issavand
204. Tehran – Majid Gheibellahi
205. Tehran – Erfan Faeqi
206. Tehran – Behzad Farhangi
207. Tehran – Majid Fallahpour
208. Tehran – Qolamreza Qazi-Zahedi
209. Tehran – Hamid Reza Qabouli
210. Tehran – ... Qorbani
211. Tehran – Payman Qolipour
212. Tehran – Mehdi Karkaee
213. Tehran – Fereidoun Kazemi
214. Tehran – Behnam Kashi
215. Tehran – Ramin Lamseh
216. Tehran – Mohammadreza Mohammadi
217. Tehran – Ahmad Morad
218. Tehran – Ali Morad-Manesh
219. Tehran – Ahmad Moradi
220. Tehran – Mehrdad Moin
221. Tehran – Majid Maleki
222. Tehran – Misagh Maleki
223. Islamshahr – Poria Naserikhah
224. Tehran – Ahmad Nazari
225. Tehran – Peyman Nouri
226. Tehran – Siamak Navidi Bildashi
227. Tehran – Hossein Niaz
228. Tehran – Hossein Niazi
229. Tehran – Mahmoud Valiollahi
230. Tehran – Hossein Yami
231. Tehran – Saeed Yousefi
232. Robat Karim – Hossein Amini
233. Robat-Karim - Hossein Aqblaqi
234. Robat Karim – Ali Babaie
235. Robat Karim – Abdolhamid Baqeri
236. Robat Karim – Naser Parvari
237. Robat Karim – Rostam Jaberi
238. Robat Karim – Farshad Jafarizadeh
239. Robat Karim – Mohsen Hosseini
240. Robat Karim – Jamshid Khodayari
241. Robat Karim – Fereydon Khosnood
242. Robat Karim – Jamal Ramazani
243. Robat Karim – Sirus Sahrvardi
244. Robat Karim – Parvaneh Saifi
245. Robat Karim – Alireza Shafaei
246. Robat Karim – Peyman Shahabi
247. Robat Karim – Alireza Zabeti
248. Robat Karim – Marzieh Abbaszadeh
249. Robat Karim – Hossein Azizi
250. Robat Karim – Mohammadreza Azizi
251. Robat Karim – Iman Fatahi
252. Robat Karim – Ebrahim Farookhi-Rad
253. Robat Karim – Farhad Forooqi
254. Robat Karim – Parvis Kashani
255. Robat Karim – Ali Kermanshahi
256. Robat Karim – Mohammad Mohebnia
257. Robat Karim – Sohrab Moqadam-Niaz-Asl
258. Robat Karim – Mohammad Mahdavi
259. Robat Karim – Javid Mirzai
260. Robat Karim – Pedram Nasseri
261. Robat Karim – Maryam Nouri
262. Robat Karim – Morteza Nouri
263. Robat Karim – Abbas Yusefi
264. Shahriar – Behrouz Asgharpour
265. Shahriar – Shahin Amiri
266. Shahriar – Mansour Eqbali
267. Shahriar – Aliollah Amini
268. Shahriar – Amin Azad
269. Shahriar – Moussa Bahram
270. Shahriar – Ayoub Bahramian
271. Shahriar – Morad Beyk
272. Shahriar – Mehdi Paapi

273. Shahriar – Omid Pakdaman
274. Shahriar – Behzad Tekieh
275. Shahriar – Mehran Jabouri
276. Shahriar – … Habibi
277. Shahriar – Reza Hassanvand
278. Shahriar – Hedayatollah Hamidi
279. Shahriar – … Dadashi
280. Shahriar – Mehdi Da'emi
281. Shahriar – Taqi Rahimi
282. Shahriar – Soleiman Rezaei
283. Shahriar – Qassem Rezai
284. Shahriar – Ali Sartipi
285. Shahriar – Mohammad Shekh-Zahed
286. Shahriar – Ehsan Shiri
287. Shahriar – Mohammad Moin Salehi
288. Shahriar – Ms. Azadeh Zarbi
289. Shahriar – Seyed-Mohammad Hossein-Tahaei
290. Shahriar – Mohammad Arabi
291. Shahriar – Mohammad Akkas
292. Shahriar – Hossein Ghadami
293. Shahriar – Ali Qorbani
294. Shahriar – Esmaeel Qolipour
295. Shahriar – Hamid Karimi
296. Shahriar – Mehdi Karimi
297. Shahriar – Mehdi Golipour
298. Shahriar – Akbar Langari
299. Shahriar – Milad Mohaqeqi
300. Shahriar – Ebrahim Mohammad-pour
301. Shahriar – Hadi Mohammad-Hosseini
302. Shahriar – Ali Mohammadian
303. Shahriar – Nader Mehdipour
304. Shahriar – Nader Momeni
305. Shahriar – Milad Nahjevand
306. Shahriar – Alireza Nouri
307. Shahriar – Mehdi Vosooqi
308. Shahriar – … Yar Mohammadi
309. Qods – Reza Einalou
310. Qods – Hossein Abroy
311. Qods – Javad Babaizadeh
312. Qods – Navid Behboodi
313. Qods – Hamid Hosseini
314. Qods – Reza Hosseini
315. Qods – Heidar Ali Ramazan-nejad
316. Qods – Hossein Shahbazi
317. Qods – Hassan Alizadeh
318. Qods – Omid Fallahati
319. Qods – Behnam UNKNOWN
320. Tehran-Kianshahr – Mohsen Karaminia
321. Mallard – Mohammad Teymouri
322. Mallard – Mohammad Khazai
323. Mallard – Milad Darvish Mohammadi
324. Mallard – Sajjad Rezai
325. Mallard – Mehrzad Rezaei
326. Mallard – Mostafa Rezaei
327. Naseem – Ahmad Hassanpour
328. Naseem – Behzad Safarzadeh
329. Varamin – Hassan Khodai
330. Yaft-Abad – Ahmad-Reza Falah
331. Yaft-Abad – Mehrdad Qassemi
332. Gonabad – Hassan Sahrai
333. Mashhad – Esmaeel Shiran
334. Mashhad – Hassan Sadati
335. Andimeshk – Seyed-Mostafa Artand
336. Andimeshk – Rahim Eskandari
337. Andimeshk – Ali Eskandari
338. Andimeshk – Shafi Baztab
339. Andimeshk – Assad Birovand
340. Andimeshk – Iman Papi
341. Andimeshk – Hojjat Lohrasbi
342. Andimeshk – Sajjad Miri
343. Andimeshk – Milad Najatvand
344. Andimeshk – Abdollah Lorestani
345. Andimeshk – Akbar Yaqoubi
346. Ahvaz – Ali Esmaeeli
347. Ahvaz – Maryam Esmaeeli
348. Ahvaz – Alireza Akbarpour
349. Ahvaz – Ali Albo-Ebadi
350. Ahvaz – Fariba Ale-Khamis
351. Ahvaz – Hamid Avi
352. Ahvaz – Shahla Baldi
353. Ahvaz – Hamzeh Bavi
354. Ahvaz – Abbas Barihi
355. Ahvaz – Mohammad Barhi (Barbehi)
356. Ahvaz – Kosar Baqlani
357. Ahvaz – Nasrin Baqlani
358. Ahvaz – Reza Beletizadeh
359. Ahvaz – Saeed Punki
360. Ahvaz – Kosar Tabe-Matouqi
361. Ahvaz – Ali Tamimi
362. Ahvaz – Amir Hosseini
363. Ahvaz – Asqar Haq-Talab

UPRISING SHAKES IRAN REGIME'S FOUNDATIONS

364. Ahvaz – Fatima Haqverdi
365. Ahvaz – Seyed-Reza Khalafzadeh
366. Ahvaz – Reza Darabpour
367. Ahvaz – Masoumeh Darabpour
368. Ahvaz – Mehdi Daris-Molai
369. Ahvaz – Kamal Daghghele
370. Ahvaz – Hassan Rabeei
371. Ahvaz – Hamid Reza-Zadeh
372. Ahvaz – Mehdi Zargani
373. Ahvaz – Bashir Sorkhi
374. Ahvaz – Hamzeh Sevari
375. Ahvaz – Reza Shahmoradi
376. Ahvaz – Hani Shahbazi
377. Ahvaz – Mehdi Abdi
378. Ahvaz – Rahim Arabpour
379. Ahvaz – Mohammad-Reza Ossafi-Zargani
380. Ahvaz – Mohsen Asakereh
381. Ahvaz – Navid Asakereh
382. Ahvaz – Amir Asakerian
383. Ahvaz – Reza Atieh Neisi
384. Ahvaz – Maryam Abdi
385. Ahvaz – Mehdi Qolamzadeh
386. Ahvaz – Soheila Fallahzadeh
387. Ahvaz – Mehdi Fallahi
388. Ahvaz – Reza Qaderi
389. Ahvaz – Mehdi Qaderi
390. Ahvaz – Farieh Karimzadeh
391. Ahvaz – Maysam Mojadam
392. Ahvaz – Seyed-Hassan Mosha'shaee
393. Ahvaz – Mobeen Moqadam
394. Ahvaz – Mohadaseh Moqadam
395. Ahvaz – Akbar Malekpour
396. Ahvaz – Reyhaneh Maleki
397. Ahvaz – Zeynab Nissanpour
398. Ahvaz – Reza Yazdani
399. Izeh – Yaser Eskandari
400. Abadan – Ravanbakhsh Emami-Rad
401. Abadan – Ravanbakhsh Emami-Malmali
402. Abadan – Mehdi Amiri
403. Abadan – Hossein Amini
404. Abadan – Ali Bavi
405. Abadan – Hamid Beshareh-Doraqi
406. Abadan – Ali Baghlani
407. Abadan – Mohammad Rezai
408. Abadan – Hossein Sajedi
409. Abadan – Zahra Sajedi
410. Abadan – Halimah Samiri
411. Abadan – Zeynab Asakereh
412. Abadan – Mehdi Asakereh
413. Abadan – Ahmad Alavi
414. Abadan – Reza Alavi
415. Abadan – Alireza Farhani
416. Abadan – Ebrahim Matouri
417. Abadan – Ali Moqadam
418. Abadan – Mehdi Moqadam
419. Behbahan – Farzad Ansari(Tazmipour)
420. Behbahan – Mohammad Hashamdar
421. Behbahan – Mahmoud Dashtinia
422. Behbahan – Mehrdad Dashtinia
423. Behbahan – Shabnam Diani
424. Behbahan – Ehsan Abdollah-Nejad
425. Behbahan – Mohammad Hossein Ghanavati
426. Behbahan – Javid Naaman
427. Hamidieh – Ahmad Sa'edi
428. Hamidieh – Shahab Siahi
429. Khorramshahr – Hassan Tamimi
430. Khorramshahr – Milad Hamidi
431. Khorramshahr – Maysam Abdolvahab-Adgipour
432. Khorramshahr – Ali Ghazlavi
433. Khorramshahr – Mohsen Mohammadpour
434. Khorramshahr – Khaled Mani'at
435. Khorramshahr – Maysam Mani'at-(Nasseri)
436. Khuzestan Province – Iman Mousavi
437. Khuzestan (Lali) – Mehdi Ahmadi
438. Dezful – Sohrab Khajeh-nouri
439. Ramhurmoz – ... Rashedi
440. Ramhurmoz – Bani Rashid
441. Ramhurmoz – Nabi Saeed
442. Ramhurmoz – Nareem Eisa
443. Ramhurmoz – Hadi Ghorbani
444. Ramhurmoz – Seyed-Hassan Moussavi
445. Ramhurmoz – Ali Moussavi
446. Shadegan – Mohsen Albuali
447. Shadegan – Bassam Alboughbaish
448. Shadegan – Ali Rashedi
449. Shush – Sadeq Kabi
450. Shushtar – Reza Delfi
451. Shushtar – Aref Delfi
452. Shushtar – Amar Zaghabi
453. Shushtar – Qassem Zaghabi

454. Shushtar – Ahmad Sa'di
455. Shushtar – Ali Soleimani
456. Shushtar – Milad Soleimani
457. Shushtar – Yas Soleimani
458. Shushtar – Mehdi Agabi
459. Shushtar – Jamal Kabi
460. Shushtar – Abbas Ka'bi
461. Shushtar – Oudi Kabi
462. Shushtar – Ali Kabi
463. Shushtar – Mamoud Ka'bi
464. Shushtar – Adel Kabi Farzeh
465. Shushtar – Ahmad-Moussavi Jo'aveleh
466. Kut Abdullah – Mojahed Alyami
467. Kut Abdullah – Hamid Movahedinejad
468. Mahshahr – Iqbal Esmaeeli
469. Mahshahr – Mansour Albavi
470. Mahshahr – Mehdi Amrai
471. Mahshahr – Khanom Omvalid
472. Mahshahr – Salem Amirsanjaran Eidani
473. Mahshahr – Yosef Albuebadi
474. Mahshahr – Ali Albughli
475. Mahshahr – Jafar Ale-Khamis
476. Mahshahr – Taher Al-Khamis
477. Mahshahr – Ghassem Bavi
478. Mahshahr – Ahad Besharat
479. Mahshahr – Amin Bechari
480. Mahshahr – Amad Cheraghian
481. Mahshahr – ... Chana'ni
482. Mahshahr – Farshad Hajipour
483. Mahshahr – Shahab Hatavi
484. Mahshahr – Mohammad Khaledi
485. Mahshahr – Youssef Khaledi
486. Mahshahr – Mohammad Khaleghi
487. Mahshahr – Ahmad Khajeh-Alboali
488. Mahshahr – Ali Khajeh-Albughli
489. Mahshahr – Mansour Daris
490. Mahshahr – Ali Rabikhah
491. Mahshahr – Hamid Sheikhani
492. Mahshahr – Mojtaba Ebadi
493. Mahshahr – Mohsen Ebadishahr
494. Mahshahr – Ms Hasineh Atighi
495. Mahshahr – Abbas(Reza) Assakereh
496. Mahshahr – Mansour Asakereh
497. Mahshahr – Majid Mojadam
498. Mahshahr – Ali Moradi
499. Mahshahr – Razzaq Nasserizadeh
500. Mahshahr – Adnan Helali
501. Masjid-Soleiman – Arman Amani
502. Zanjan – Amir-Hossein Abbasi
503. Garmsar – Mohammad-Amin Alikai
504. Garmsar – Kourosh Shahlai
505. Garmsar – Hassan Tavoosi
506. Garmsar – Hamid Qobakhlou
507. Shiraz – Sadeq Ahmad-Panahi
508. Shiraz – Janfeshan Assadi
509. Shiraz – Nader Assadi
510. Shiraz – Amir Alvandi
511. Shiraz – Seyed-Alireza Anjavi
512. Shiraz – Hossein Bazrafshan
513. Shiraz – ... Parsai
514. Shiraz – ... Parsai
515. Shiraz – Mohsen Pydar
516. Shiraz – Amir Panahi
517. Shiraz – Ahmad-Reza Pour-Qayoumi
518. Shiraz – Rassoul Shirvani
519. Shiraz – Vahid Torabi
520. Shiraz – Mohammad Tavasoli
521. Shiraz – Vahid Tavasoli
522. Shiraz – Mehdi Janbazi
523. Shiraz – Bahman Jafari
524. Shiraz – Mohammad-Reza Jamshidi
525. Shiraz – Mehdi Jahanbazi
526. Shiraz – Mohammad-Hossein Hourang
527. Shiraz – Hossein Heidari
528. Shiraz – Mohammadreza Khorshidi
529. Shiraz – Mohammad-Hossein Dastankhah
530. Shiraz – Reza Dehqan
531. Shiraz – Amir Roodgari
532. Shiraz – Hamid Reyhani
533. Shiraz – Majid Reyhani
534. Shiraz – Hashem Zare
535. Shiraz – Mostafa Zamani
536. Shiraz – Sadeq Sa'adat
537. Shiraz – Mehdi Soluki
538. Shiraz – Mohammad Shojaee
539. Shiraz – Payman Shoaian
540. Shiraz – Mohammad-Hossein Shekari
541. Shiraz – Saeed Sadeqi
542. Shiraz – Reza Alipour
543. Shiraz – Hamid Farhadi
544. Shiraz – Amir Pasha Qarchivand
545. Shiraz – Kambiz Qardashi

546. Shiraz – Kianoush Qardashi
547. Shiraz – Jamal Qoreishi
548. Shiraz – Morteza Mohammadzadegan
549. Shiraz – Mehdi Moqadamzadeh
550. Shiraz – Farshad Miri
551. Shiraz – Nader Nasirpour
552. Shiraz – Javad Nekoui
553. Shiraz – Mehdi (Ali) Nekoui Abadi
554. Shiraz – Majid Hashemi
555. Shiraz – Seyed-Keyvan Yarfi
556. Shiraz – Mohammad Yousefi
557. Safashahr – Mohammad-Hossein Nazari
558. Shiraz-Kelar – Rassoul Ghavami
559. Marvdasht – Mehdi Nikoui
560. Qazvin – Mojtaba Gheydari
561. Sanandaj – Pouya Ahmadzadeh
562. Sanandaj – Mohammad-Reza Ahmadi
563. Sanandaj – Massoud Amini
564. Sanandaj – Ali Baghlani
565. Sanandaj – Ali Javaheri
566. Sanandaj – Ziba Khoshgvar
567. Sanandaj – Ershad Rahmanian
568. Sanandaj – Hiva Rahimi
569. Sanandaj – Nasser Rahzai
570. Sanandaj – Mozzafar Seifi
571. Sanandaj – ... Shahoo
572. Sanandaj – Reza Sadeqi
573. Sanandaj – ... Fa'eq
574. Sanandaj – Ahmad Reza Mohammadi
575. Sanandaj – Souran Mohammadi
576. Sanandaj – Kaveh Veysani
577. Marivan – Usman Ahmadi
578. Marivan – Danial Ostovari
579. Marivan – Saman Bassami
580. Marivan – Edris Bivareh
581. Marivan – Mehran Taak
582. Marivan – Aryaan Rajabi
583. Marivan – Behrouz Maleki
584. Marivan – Usman Naderi
585. Sirjan – Ruhollah Nazari-Fat'habadi
586. Islamabad-Qarb – Saeed Nurollahi
587. Javanroud – Arash Ayobi
588. Javanroud – Jabbar Tejareh
589. Javanroud – Farshad Kheirandish
590. Javanroud – Salman Rahmani
591. Javanroud – Khaled Rashidi
592. Javanroud – Kaveh Rezai
593. Javanroud – Ribvar Seyed-Rostami
594. Javanroud – Mobin Abdollahi
595. Javanroud – Bahram Qolami
596. Javanroud – Ali(Yunes) Firouzbakht
597. Javanroud – Kaveh Mohammadi
598. Javanroud – Ebrahim Moradi
599. Javanroud – Hashem Moradi
600. Javanroud – Hamzeh Naghdi
601. Javanroud – Yunes Houshangi
602. Sanqar – Mohammad Heydarian
603. Kermanshah – Hamid Cheraghi
604. Kermanshah – Massoud Ebrahimi
605. Kermanshah – Saeed Ershadi
606. Kermanshah – Mojtaba Esfandiar-Sabet
607. Kermanshah – Mohsen Esfandiari
608. Kermanshah – Saeed Esmaeelian
609. Kermanshah – Saeed Esmaeeli
610. Kermanshah – Ali Alqasi
611. Kermanshah – Vahid Elahi
612. Kermanshah – Saeed Amiri
613. Kermanshah – Behnam Amirian
614. Kermanshah – Hossein Amini
615. Kermanshah – Hessam Barani-Rad
616. Kermanshah – Mostafa Bakeri
617. Kermanshah – Hamid Borhani
618. Kermanshah – Qader Bahmanyar
619. Kermanshah – Sajjad Biranvand
620. Kermanshah – Shakiba Biranvand
621. Kermanshah – Nader Biravand
622. Kermanshah – Saeed Bayj
623. Kermanshah – Nader Bijanvand
624. Kermanshah – Abolfazl Bigdeli
625. Kermanshah – Javad Palani
626. Kermanshah – Mohammad Palani
627. Kermanshah – Farshad Palevani
628. Kermanshah – Valiollah Pir-Hayati
629. Kermanshah – Nader Rezaei Abtaaf
630. Kermanshah – Qolam Tabzar
631. Kermanshah – Saber Tavasolkani
632. Kermanshah – Farshad Tavakoli
633. Kermanshah – Farrokh Jabbari
634. Kermanshah – Hojat Jalali
635. Kermanshah – Afshin Jalili
636. Kermanshah – Yunes Jalili
637. Kermanshah – Ali Javanroudi

638. Kermanshah – Foad Joshan
639. Kermanshah – Behzad Jooybareh
640. Kermanshah – Nemat Hosseini
641. Kermanshah – Javad Haydari
642. Kermanshah – Esmat Haydari
643. Kermanshah – Esmaeel Kharmand
644. Kermanshah – Alireza Damvandi
645. Kermanshah – Gholamreza Davoudi
646. Kermanshah – Faramarz Rahimi
647. Kermanshah – Mohammad-Javad Rostami
648. Kermanshah – Mazaher Rostami
649. Kermanshah – Mohammad Rasouli
650. Kermanshah – Saeed Rezai
651. Kermanshah – Mahmoud Rezai
652. Kermanshah – Mansour Rezai
653. Kermanshah – Rassoul Ziarati-Khoshnam
654. Kermanshah – Sadra Sarbaleh
655. Kermanshah – Ahmad Shakeri
656. Kermanshah – Abdollah Shahabadi
657. Kermanshah – Vida Shakibai-Moqadam
658. Kermanshah – Milad Shirazi
659. Kermanshah – Abdolreza Shirzadi
660. Kermanshah – Sadeq Abbasi-Kordnia
661. Kermanshah – Farshid Ezzatshahi
662. Kermanshah – Yunes Ezzati
663. Kermanshah – Hashem Ezzatipour
664. Kermanshah – Bahman Azizi
665. Kermanshah – Yunes Eini
666. Kermanshah – Rostam Eivaz-zadeh
667. Kermanshah – Ali Qafoori
668. Kermanshah – Ali Qolampour
669. Kermanshah – Manouchehr Fathi
670. Kermanshah – Vahid Fathi
671. Kermanshah – Mansour Fakhri
672. Kermanshah – Ibrahim Fadai
673. Kermanshah – Hamzeh Faraji
674. Kermanshah – Mamoud Fardpour
675. Kermanshah – Mostafa Farzami
676. Kermanshah – Behrouz Farhadpour
677. Kermanshah – Behrouz Fallahi Raad
678. Kermanshah – Moslem Fayazi
679. Kermanshah – Armin Qaderi
680. Kermanshah – Farzad Qassemi-Moghaddam
681. Kermanshah – Hedayat Qorbani
682. Kermanshah – Jamshid Kazemi
683. Kermanshah – Bahman Kamrani
684. Kermanshah – Javad Karami
685. Kermanshah – Khosro Karimi
686. Kermanshah – Houshang Karimi
687. Kermanshah – Farhad Majidi
688. Kermanshah – Danial Mohammadi
689. Kermanshah – Reza Mahmoodi
690. Kermanshah – Javad Mokhtari
691. Kermanshah – Heshmat Moradi
692. Kermanshah – Masoud Moradi
693. Kermanshah – Eskandar Mortazavi
694. Kermanshah – Borhan Mansournia
695. Kermanshah – Ahmad Mansouri
696. Kermanshah – Abdollah Mansouri
697. Kermanshah – Ali-Asghar Molania
698. Kermanshah – Majid Assad-Molania
699. Kermanshah – Mohammad Mirzai
700. Kermanshah – Mohammad Naderi
701. Kermanshah – Mohammad-Reza Nobakhti-Nia
702. Kermanshah – Mostafa Hemmatirad
703. Kermanshah – Mozzafar Vatandoust
704. Kermanshah – Nima Karimi
705. Gorgan – Hamed Semnani
706. Rasht – Mohsen Nezamdoost
707. Somesara – … Kiaei
708. Langaroud – Pejman (Ali) Gholipour
709. Khorramabad – Hossein Paapi
710. Khorramabad – Arshia Pirouzi
711. Khorramabad – Farshad Darikvand
712. Khorramabad – Seyed-Mostafa Zare'zadeh
713. Khorramabad – Morteza Moradi
714. Khorramabad – Omid Mohammad Mehrabi
715. Arak – Ali Assadi
716. Arak – Massoud Saberi
717. Arak – Farhad Miri
718. Saveh – Mohammad-Ali Bahramian
719. Saveh – Esmaeel Shojaee
720. Saveh – Aboulfazl Sha'bani
721. Minab – Hossein Torkamani
722. Minab – Mohammad Jalali
723. Bandar Abbas – Qassem Khaladeh
724. Bandar Abbas – Moussa Shojaei

Children Murdered in Iran Protests * November 2019

 Reza Abdullahi, 13
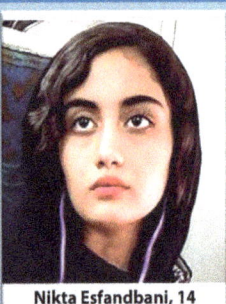 Nikta Esfandbani, 14
 Mohammad Dastan-Khah, 15
 Armin Ghaderi, 15
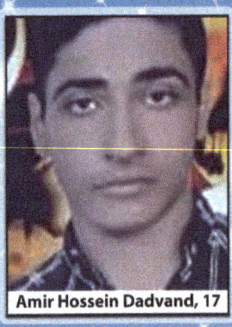 Amir Hossein Dadvand, 17
 Mohammad Berihi, 17
 Sasab Eidivand, 17
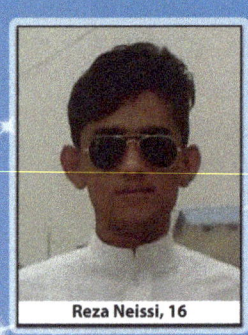 Reza Neissi, 16
 Hessam Barani Rad
 Ahmad M. Jo'avaleh, 17
 Alireza Noori, 17
 Mohsen Mohammadpour, 17
 Reza Moazzami, 18
 Pejman Gholipour, under 18
 Pedram Jafari, 18
 Mohammad Taheri, 17

List of publications

List of Publications by the National Council of Resistance of Iran, U.S. Representative Office

Iran's Emissaries of Terror

June 2019, 208 pages

This book explains the extent to which Tehran's embassies and diplomats are at the core of both the planning and execution of international terrorism targeting Iranian dissidents, as well as central to Tehran's direct and proxy terrorism against other countries.

Iran Doubles Down on Terror and Turmoil

November 2018, 63 pages

This book examines the regime's political and economic strategy, which revolves around terrorism and physical annihilation of opponents. Failing to quell growing popular protests, Tehran has bolstered domestic suppression with blatant terrorism and intimidation.

Iran Will Be Free:
Speech by Maryam Rajavi

September 2018, 54 pages

Text of a keynote speech delivered by Mrs. Maryam Rajavi on June 30, 2018, at the Iranian Resistance's grand gathering in Paris, France explaining the path to freedom in Iran and what she envisions for future Iran.

Iran's Ballistic Buildup: The March Toward Nuclear-Capable Missiles

May 2018, 136 pages

This manuscript surveys Iran's missile capabilities, including the underlying organization, structure, production, and development infrastructure, as well as launch facilities and the command centers. The book exposes the nexus between the regime's missile activities and its nuclear weapons program, including ties with North Korea.

Iran: Cyber Repression: How the IRGC Uses Cyberwarfare to Preserve the Theocracy

February 2018, 70 pages

This manuscript demonstrates how the Iranian regime, under the supervision and guidance of the IRGC and the Ministry of Intelligence and Security (MOIS), have employed new cyberwarfare and tactics in a desperate attempt to counter the growing dissent inside the country.

Iran: Where Mass Murderers Rule: The 1988 Massacre of 30,000 Political Prisoners and the Continuing Atrocities

November 2017, 161 pages

Iran: Where Mass Murderers Rule is an expose of the current rulers of Iran and their track record in human rights violations. The book details how 30,000 political prisoners fell victim to politicide during the summer of 1988 and showcases the egregious political extinction of a group of people.

Iran's Nuclear Core: Uninspected Military Sites, Vital to the Nuclear Weapons Program

October 2017, 52 pages

This book details how the nuclear weapons program is at the heart of, and not parallel to, the civil nuclear program of Iran. The program has been run by the Islamic Revolutionary Guards Corp (IRGC) since the beginning, and the main nuclear sites and nuclear research facilities have been hidden from the eyes of the United Nations nuclear watchdog.

Terrorist Training Camps in Iran: How Islamic Revolutionary Guards Corps Trains Foreign Fighters to Export Terrorism

June 2017, 56 pages

The book details how Islamic Revolutionary Guards Corps trains foreign fighters in 15 various camps in Iran to export terrorism. The IRGC has created a large directorate within its extraterritorial arm, the Quds Force, in order to expand its training of foreign mercenaries as part of the strategy to step up its meddling abroad in Syria, Iraq, Yemen, Bahrain, Afghanistan and elsewhere.

Presidential Elections in Iran: Changing Faces; Status Quo Policies

May 2017, 78 pages

The book reviews the past 11 presidential elections, demonstrating that the only criterion for qualifying as a candidate is practical and heartfelt allegiance to the Supreme Leader. An unelected vetting watchdog, the Guardian Council makes that determination.

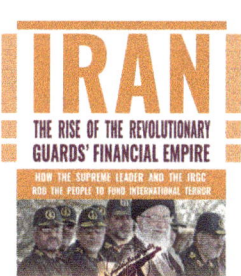

The Rise of Iran's Revolutionary Guards' Financial Empire: How the Supreme Leader and the IRGC Rob the People to Fund International Terror

March 2017, 174 pages

This study shows how ownership of property in various spheres of the economy is gradually shifted from the population writ large towards a minority ruling elite comprised of the Supreme Leader's office and the IRGC, using 14 powerhouses, and how the money ends up funding terrorism worldwide.

UPRISING SHAKES IRAN REGIME'S FOUNDATIONS

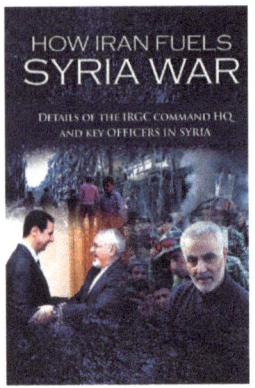

How Iran Fuels Syria War: Details of the IRGC Command HQ and Key Officers in Syria
November 2016, 74 pages

This book examines how the Iranian regime has effectively engaged in the military occupation of Syria by marshaling 70,000 forces, including the Islamic Revolutionary Guard Corps (IRGC) and mercenaries from other countries into Syria; is paying monthly salaries to over 250,000 militias and agents to prolong the conflict; and divided the country into 5 zones of conflict, establishing 18 command, logistics and operations centers.

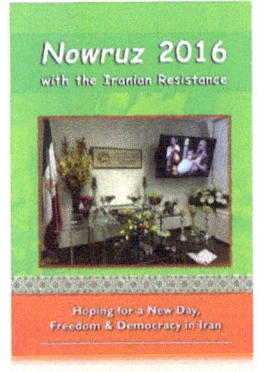

Nowruz 2016 with the Iranian Resistance: Hoping for a New Day, Freedom and Democracy in Iran
April 2016, 36 pages

This book describes Iranian New Year, Nowruz celebrations at the Washington office of Iran's parliament-in-exile, the National Council of Resistance of Iran. The yearly event marks the beginning of spring. It includes select speeches by dignitaries who have attended the NCRIUS Nowruz celebrations.

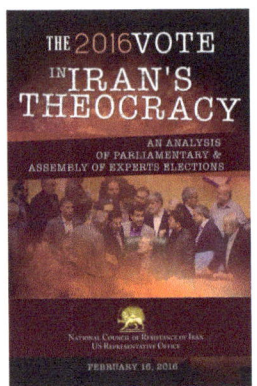

The 2016 Vote in Iran's Theocracy: An analysis of Parliamentary & Assembly of Experts Elections
February 2016, 70 pages

This book examines all the relevant data about the 2016 Assembly of Experts as well as Parliamentary elections ahead of the February 2016 elections. It looks at the history of elections since the revolution in 1979 and highlights the current intensified infighting among the various factions of the Iranian regime.

IRAN: A Writ of Deception and Cover-up: Iranian Regime's Secret Committee Hid Military Dimensions of its Nuclear Program
February 2016, 30 pages

The book provides details about a top-secret committee in charge of forging response to the International Atomic Energy Agency (IAEA) regarding the Possible Military Dimensions (PMD) of Tehran's nuclear program, including those related to the detonators called EBW (Exploding Bridge Wire), an integral part of developing an implosion type nuclear device.

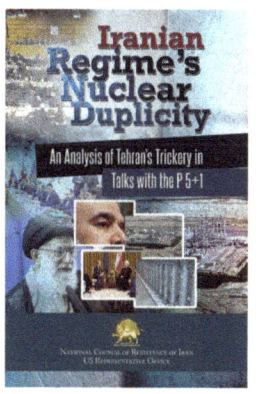

Iranian Regime's Nuclear Duplicity: An Analysis of Tehran's Trickery in Talks with the P 5+1

January 2016, 74 pages

This book examines Iran's behavior throughout the negotiations process in an effort to inform the current dialogue on a potential agreement. Drawing on both publicly available sources and those within Iran, the book focuses on two major periods of intense negotiations with the regime: 2003-2004 and 2013-2015.

Key to Countering Islamic Fundamentalism: Maryam Rajavi? Testimony To The U.S. House Foreign Affairs Committee

June 2015, 68 pages

Testimony before U.S. House Foreign Affairs Committee's subcommittee on Terrorism, non-Proliferation, and Trade discussing ISIS and Islamic fundamentalism. The book contains Maryam Rajavi's full testimony as well as the question and answer by representatives.

Meet the National Council of Resistance of Iran

June 2014, 150 pages

Meet the National Council of Resistance of Iran discusses what NCRI stands for, what its platform is, and why a vision for a free, democratic, secular, non-nuclear republic in Iran would serve world peace.

How Iran Regime Cheated the World: Tehran's Systematic Efforts to Cover Up its Nuclear Weapons Program

June 2014, 50 pages

The monograph discusses the Iranian regime's report card as far as it relates to being transparent when addressing the international community's concerns about the true nature and the ultimate purpose of its nuclear program.

About the NCRI-US

The National Council of Resistance of Iran-US Representative Office (NCRI-US) acts as the Washington office for Iran's parliament-in-exile, the National Council of Resistance of Iran, which is dedicated to the establishment of a democratic, secular, non-nuclear republic in Iran.

NCRI-US, registered as a non-profit tax-exempt organization, has been instrumental in exposing the nuclear weapons program of Iran, including the sites in Natanz, and Arak, the biological and chemical weapons program of Iran, as well as its ambitious ballistic missile program.

NCRI-US has also exposed the terrorist network of the regime, including its involvement in the bombing of Khobar Towers in Saudi Arabia, the Jewish Community Center in Argentina, its fueling of sectarian violence in Iraq and Syria, and its malign activities in other parts of the Middle East.

Our office has provided information on the human rights violations in Iran, extensive anti-government demonstrations, and the movement for democratic change in Iran.

Visit our website at www.ncrius.org

You may follow us on   twitter   @ncrius

Follow us on   facebook   NCRIUS

You can also find us on   Instagram   NCRIUS

www.ingramcontent.com/pod-product-compliance
Lightning Source LLC
Chambersburg PA
CBHW040223040426
42333CB00051B/3420